When LIFE *comes* UNDONE

Timothy J. Addington

T.J. ADDINGTON
with
MARY ANN ADDINGTON

When
LIFE
comes
UNDONE

**Walking in Faith When Life Is
Hard and Hope Is Scarce**

BookVillages

When Life Comes Undone: Walking in Faith When Life Is Hard and Hope Is Scarce

© 2011 by T.J. Addington

ISBN: 978-1-93851-200-1

Cover design by Niddy Griddy Design, Inc.
Cover photo © istock

LCCN: 2012939213

Printed in the United States of America

16 15 14 13 12 / 2 3 4 5 6 7 8 9

This book is dedicated with love to Arthur and Karen Ellison and Wayne and Jan Kaufman, friends who have walked with our family when life was hard and hope was scarce. Your faithful ministry to us through prayer and friendship for many years has been a priceless gift.

To our amazing sons, Jon and Steven (Chip),
who displayed courage and faith when their father was near death.

To our "Friends for Life" who have loved us so faithfully;
you know who you are.

And to each one who joined in praying
for my life
and healing.

CONTENTS

ACKNOWLEDGMENTS

Mary Ann and I are deeply indebted to each person who agreed to share their stories so that you could be encouraged. Each one has shared in the "fellowship of His suffering" and walked in faith through hard times. Along with the heroes of Hebrews 11, they are champions of God's transforming grace. Their scars are divine scars, and God's comfort that flowed into their lives overflows into the lives of others. We also thank our friends and publishers at Dawson Media for their help in making this book a reality, and my editor, Darla Hightower, for her diligence with the manuscript and to Karen Pickering of Dawson Media for shepherding the entire process.

INTRODUCTION

Life has come undone. One day life is normal, and the next day our lives are thrown into confusion and chaos. Like a drowning person, we find ourselves fighting to get back to the surface so we can take a breath. Pain, fear, and uncertainty have taken over. It is hard to even grasp this new reality as our minds and hearts shout, "This cannot be!"

If any of this describes you, a friend, or family member, this book is written for you. This is an authentic experience with life and pain and faith. Ultimately, this book offers hope for what can be after life has come undone, but before we get to what *can be* we must deal with *what is*. We must struggle through the emotional turmoil when life's rules change cruelly without our permission.

No matter how strong our faith, such events often create a crisis of faith. To *not* ask hard questions about God's love and faithfulness in the trauma of life undone is abnormal, maybe irrational. Never is our understanding of God's love, grace, and mercy more challenged and the answers more important than when life is hard and hope is scarce. We hang on to faith by the tips of our fingers as our minds work to encompass issues we have never had to understand except in a theoretical way.

To all of this there are no easy answers and often just more questions. The life undone forces us to question and reexamine the very core of what faith and life are about. I have asked these hard questions, and I am sure you have as well.

I invite you on a journey toward a life of hope, wholeness, and freedom. You can get there, regardless of how your life has come undone. This is not a journey of easy answers but one of honest realities, unlikely gifts, divine scars, God's goodness, and ultimately a freedom that you have never experienced before.

There is nothing theoretical about *When Life Comes Undone*. It comes out of real life, real pain, real struggle, and real faith. It explores the question, How do we walk by faith when life is hard and hope is scarce? Where is God in our pain? Why does God allow life to come undone when I have served Him and followed Him? There are no easy answers, but there are divine perspectives that can help us on that hard journey we all walk at one time or another.

I have walked this hard path. Walk with me toward freedom.

When life comes undone, having a community of support becomes crucial. You may choose to use this book in a small group with others who are on this journey. Finding your freedom may involve receiving from others as well as giving your compassion and prayer to others. Use the discussion questions at the end of each chapter in your small group. Each chapter also includes a prayer, as an example of praying boldly. I invite you to prayerfully read through this book, allowing God to minister to your heart and heal your pain.

CHAPTER ONE

LIFE UNDONE
When Life Changes Forever

Like a tsunami breaking over our lives, it washes over us bringing fear, shock, and uncertainty—and we know that our lives are forever changed. In its wake, the landscape of our lives is left rearranged and unfamiliar, and our brains struggle to make sense of a new and unfamiliar reality.

The doctor tells you that it is cancer. Life comes undone.

A husband announces that he is no longer in love with you and he will be filing for divorce. Life comes undone.

A call comes at midnight telling you that your daughter has been in an accident and you are needed at the hospital now. Life comes undone.

After years in a successful career you have been notified that your job has been eliminated. Life comes undone.

The bank informs you that you no longer qualify for a business loan, and you are forced to file for bankruptcy. Life comes undone.

In the economic downturn your retirement account is now worth half of what it was and you cannot retire. Life comes undone.

You discover your spouse is having an affair and in fact has been living a double life for years. Life comes undone.

Your sixteen-year-old son committed suicide. Life comes undone in the most painful and permanent way possible.

Your parents tell you that they love you but not each other. They are separating. Life comes undone.

You come to grips with the fact that you were sexually abused as a child. Life comes undone.

In a thousand different ways, public and private, life comes undone—leaving us in shock, scrambling to understand why, and coping with new challenges. Since you are reading this book, my guess is that you know exactly what I mean. If you don't, you will, because everyone eventually has a life-comes-undone experience.

Every day I am reminded that life has come undone for someone as I receive CaringBridge updates from families desperate for prayer and a miracle for a loved one in dire need.

I think of Josh, the eighteen-year-old, who recently became a paraplegic in a skiing accident and is grappling with a future in a wheelchair. His life landscape is dramatically different than it was just four months ago. I pray daily for Ashley, recovering from a car accident two months ago with unknown challenges ahead of her. Every time life comes undone the ripples are felt by families, friends, and loved ones.

The question is not *if* life will come undone but *when*. And when it does, how do we respond? Where do we gain perspective for our new reality? Where is God in our pain? Where do we find hope?

This is a book of reality, perspective, and hope. Life will come undone, but God does not! Life will come undone, but God's purposes for our lives do not change. There is life *after* life undone. Life is different but in many ways richer than before because the divine scars we wear give us new perspective, new faith, and new resolve—if we allow it. In fact, it is often the pain and scars of a life undone that drives us to explore life with Jesus more closely. When there is nowhere else to turn, He is there, waiting.

If this is your life right now, this book will encourage you in the midst of your discouragement and give you divine hope. God is the ultimate source of hope. He is our secure Rock, and in Him we have both hope for the future and what we need in the moment—if we allow Him to infuse our despair with His presence. As Jesus said in John 10:10, "The thief comes only to steal and kill and destroy; I have come that they [you] may have life, and have it to the full." That is God's heart for us.

How we respond to life undone determines whether we emerge from our dark night of the soul with greater depth of heart and faith. If not, we allow ourselves to descend into despair, discouragement, and sadness. I choose the former!

I invite you to join me on the journey from life undone to life redone. It is a journey of pain, discovery, faith, joy, God's grace, and finally freedom.

INDELIBLE MOMENTS

Most of us remember exactly where we were when we heard about the twin towers on 9/11. As my son Jon and I watched the second tower collapse he said, "I was born into one world. This is a different world." He knew that a seismic shift had taken place in our nation. Massive events have a way of imprinting themselves indelibly on our consciousness. The same is true in our personal histories when life comes undone. In big and small ways we are forever changed and the landscape of our lives forever different. If you have been there, you know!

One of my former colleagues experienced one of those indelible moments a few weeks ago. His e-mail to me says it all: "Recently a battery of tests led to this pronouncement from my neurologist: 'You are in the early stages of Alzheimer's disease.' Believe me, Tim, this was quite a shock. Several weeks later, it still is."

My friend knows—his family knows—that life will never be the same. And that the cruel disease of Alzheimer's will slowly rob a brilliant mind of its ability to reason or remember. For his family, that visit to the neurologist changes everything forever. And this prognosis has no cure—it is a one-way street. This is life coming undone bit by bit, day by day, with the cruelty of knowing it is happening, until one is robbed of all understanding and the pain is borne by loved ones and friends.

December 4, 2007, is one of those indelibly imprinted dates for my family. I woke that morning unable to breathe with great pain in my chest and sides. I'm not one to easily go to the doctor, so my wife, Mary Ann, was surprised when I readily agreed to go to the emergency room. I knew I was in trouble. But I had no idea how much trouble I was in and that I should have never left the hospital alive.

As soon as a bed was available, I was sent to the intensive care unit (ICU), where I would stay for thirty-two days with massive pneumonia.

Within a week I had only 30 percent of my lung capacity available for breathing, as the other 70 percent was filled with fluid. But the medical professionals could not diagnose the cause, and the antibiotics were not working to stem the slide into a critical life-threatening situation.

Because breathing was so difficult and the pain so severe, they decided to put me into a drug-induced coma, intubate me, and put me on a ventilator as they tried to determine the cause of the pneumonia. After a week in the ICU the doctors were able to discover the cause—a highly dreaded and difficult to treat MRSA pneumonia (Methicillin-Resistant Staphylococcus Aureus). They started to treat it with a cocktail of antibiotics that they hoped would work fast enough for me to survive.

But the treatment was not to be easy. I had already developed pleural effusion (fluid in the lining of the lungs), and about 800cc was drained from the lining of my lungs and the chest wall. Simultaneously, congestive heart failure set in since my heart could not keep up with the fluid build-up. At the same time, fluid continued to build in my lungs (pulmonary edema), which led to respiratory failure and eighteen days on a ventilator.

The consequences of these complications led to ARDS (acute respiratory distress syndrome), a severe inflammatory process in the lungs where one starts to drown in his own fluids. Septic shock set in (infection that takes over the whole body) and there was not an adequate blood supply to my major organs. If that was not enough, the mitral valve in my heart failed, which led to my heart not being able to pump properly (usually a fatal situation unless repaired by immediate open heart surgery, which I would not have survived).

The stresses on my heart caused atrial fibrillation, where my heart tried to compensate for the congestive heart failure, mitral valve regurgitation, and septic shock. My heart was beating at 240 beats per minute, and two chest shocks ("clear") failed to bring the heart rate down.

Just to keep life interesting I also developed encephalopathy (brain inflammation) from the physiological assault on my body, and for a while the medical staff were concerned about brain damage.

It would be forty-two days in the hospital, thirty-two of them in intensive care, and six weeks after my discharge before I could go back to work—and then only part time. Eighteen months later I am still in physical therapy for various issues resulting from that long hospital stay that I never should have survived.

Life came undone for our family on December 4, 2007, and it would continue to do so for the next eighteen months, including another two-week hospital stay on a ventilator—this time in Thailand (that story later). I am sure that you, too, can pinpoint a date or dates when life came undone and everything changed for you. Life does that to all of us.

NEVER THE SAME

The images of the before and after pictures of the tsunami in Aceh, Indonesia, will never leave me. It is amazing how different the after pictures are from the before pictures. Whole land areas disappeared and then new areas reappeared. The tsunami literally rearranged the landscape and geography of the region.

That is the picture of life undone. We wake up one morning and realize that life is different and will never be the same again. For some, the changes are permanent and major.

When Josh went skiing on a March day in 2009, as he had dozens of times before, he could not have imagined the accident that would sever his spinal cord and leave him a paraplegic. This strapping eighteen-year-old outdoors kid found himself in a hospital hearing that he has a permanent injury. They needed to put two steel braces in his back to stabilize it, and then he faced weeks of hospital care and rehabilitation, learning what it means to live with wheels instead of legs. Six months later he is still learning what it means to live with wheels, how to get around, dealing with the loss of all the things he once took for granted, and wondering what purpose God might have in allowing this accident to happen.

The emotional toll on Josh and his family has been intense. His parents' lives became all about survival as they tried to process and help Josh process his new reality. Their strong faith in God was tested daily as they grappled with why this happened to their son. The fatigue of just surviving took a long and hard toll. Their questions are no less than their son's.

They, too, must deal with dreams lost, and as parents they long to make Josh physically whole again but they cannot. His dad, a pastor, struggles to answer the tough questions that he often preached on, but now he must ask them, and the answers are tough to come by. There are no easy answers, and the often glib phrases of others cause additional pain rather than hope. One day there is encouragement and the next day renewed sorrow. One day there is an encouraging step forward and the next they are back in the emergency room for an infection. Every day is a challenge for the whole family. Life will never be the same as it was—that is the nature of life undone.

Like me, they emerge from their dark night of the soul different, changed, but with hope and faith, and a growing measure of peace that God has a plan even in the midst of their trauma and that they can trust Him for their future. The geography and landscape of their lives has changed significantly and forever, but the God they trust has not changed and that fact changes everything.

When Mary Ann and I were married some thirty-three years ago at the tender age of twenty, we did so with great dreams and unlimited optimism. Years later we have a deeper love, but we are different people, forged in the heat of the events of life that changed the landscape of our lives in ways we could never have imagined. We would never have intentionally "signed up" for some of what we have faced. There has been great joy and great pain—all of which has created a new me and a new her and a new us.

A DIVINE PERSPECTIVE

Many people have asked me, "Why do you think this happened to you?" My answer is, "Why would it *not* happen to me?" Life comes undone for us all. It's part of living in a world that rebelled against God when Adam and Eve chose to go their own way and disobey Him, and each of us has participated in that rebellion.

That does not mean that our troubles are God's punishment for our sin. He has no need to punish us since He took our sin on Himself when He died on the cross. All we need to do is accept His death on our behalf and He forgives us our sin. "For God so loved the world that he gave his one and only Son, that whoever believes in him shall not perish but have eternal life. For God did not send his Son into the world to condemn the world, but to save the world through him. Whoever believes in him is not condemned." (John 3:16-18)

We suffer because we live in a broken, fallen world where disease exists, death comes, people mistreat people, nations go to war, justice is often scarce, natural disasters disrupt, famine and drought come, wars rage, and the list could go on. All of this the result of sin, which infected the garden in the beginning and will exist until Jesus comes back to establish His perfect kingdom.

Jesus made this point clear to His disciples on the eve of His death on the cross. "I have told you these things, so that in me you may have peace. In this world you will have trouble. But take heart! I have overcome the world" (John 16:33).

There are many who believe that as followers of Jesus we should not experience pain, sickness, poverty, or other realities of life in this world. But what do you make of Jesus' words, "In this world you *will* have trouble" (emphasis added). That is a defining statement—and one that all of us know to be true. There will come a day when God will redeem this sinful, fallen, and troubled world, but that day is yet to come. In the meantime, we live with the results of the rebellion against God in the garden and none of us will escape the troubles that the world brings.

At the same time, Jesus says, "in me you may have peace." You won't escape trouble, suffering, hardship, pain, hurt, difficulty, but "*in me* you may have peace" (emphasis added) in spite of those things. That is a game changer! How many people do you know who have a sense of peace in the middle of their pain or suffering? I know a few, and their sense of peace in the midst of their difficulty is a magnet to others who want to know where that peace comes from.

Actually, we need to look at some of the previous words of Jesus to understand that peace because He said "I have told you these things, so that in me you may have peace" (John 16:33). What "things" is Jesus referring to? They are key things about Himself that He had shared previously with His disciples. As you read these statements of Jesus think about your situation and what they mean for you today:

- For God so loved the world that he gave his one and only Son, that whoever believes in him shall not perish but have eternal life. (John 3:16)
- Whoever believes in the Son has eternal life. (John 3:36)
- Whoever hears my word and believes him who sent me has eternal life and will not be condemned; he has crossed over from death to life. (John 5:24)
- I am the bread of life. He who comes to me will never go hungry, and he who believes in me will never be thirsty. (John 6:35)
- I am the light of the world. Whoever follows me will never walk in darkness, but will have the light of life. (John 8:12)
- If you hold to my teaching, you are really my disciples. Then you will know that truth, and the truth will set you free. (John 8:31-32)
- I have come that they may have life, and have it to the full. (John 10:10)
- I am the resurrection and the life. He who believes in me will live, even though he dies; and whoever lives and believes in me will never die. (John 11:25-26)
- I have come into the world as a light, so that no one who believes in me should stay in darkness. (John 12:46)
- I am the way and the truth and the life. No one comes to the Father except through me. (John 14:6)
- Peace I leave with you; my peace I give you. I do not give to you as the world gives. Do not let your hearts be troubled and do not be afraid. (John 14:27)

These are amazing statements of God's goodness to us. He forgives our sin, He promises us eternal life with Him when we die, we no longer need to live with the guilt of our mistakes and failures, He gives us meaning and purpose, provides us with direction, gives us freedom that comes through knowing Him and His truth, grants us fullness of life, and through Him we know the God of the universe. No wonder He can say, "Peace I leave with you; my peace I give you" (John 14:27).

That is also why Jesus can say, "I have told you these things, so that in me you may have peace. In this world you will have trouble. But take heart! I have overcome the world" (John 16:33). Jesus gives us three improbable statements in tandem. You can have peace; you will have trouble; I have overcome the world. The fact that we will have trouble in this life is sandwiched between two unlikely statements: In me [Jesus] you may have peace and I [Jesus] have overcome the world.

Our peace is not found in our positive thinking, our ability to control our situation, even our knowledge that our situation will go away and our pain be removed. No, it is found in the *person* of Jesus Christ. Our peace is not a result of our circumstances but of the person of Jesus and His presence in the midst of our pain, uncertainty, and difficulty. We have this peace *if* we will allow Him into our lives and ask for His presence. He does not force Himself on us.

Jesus also says, "I have overcome the world." In our pain and suffering—when life comes undone—in our dark night of the soul—it is easy to believe that pain, suffering, injustice, sadness, or sorrow won.

Jesus says, NO! It may not appear that way at the moment, but I am God. I not only died for the sin and brokenness of the world but I rose from the grave triumphant, and one day I will return and make all that is wrong in our world right, bringing healing, justice, joy, righteousness, and peace to a world that desperately needs all of these. And even now, I can break through the trouble you face, and My presence can be your hope and your peace.

If God has overcome the world, He has overcome the pain and sorrow you presently face, even though it does not seem apparent in the moment. This will become evident as you work your way through this book. We live with our present pain in the knowledge that God has already overcome that pain, and that there is coming a day when all will be made right.

We have the assurance that in spite of our circumstances today we can live with the peace of God—a supernatural gift found in the person of Jesus Christ, who infuses our suffering and pain with His presence and light. He does not leave us alone but *joins* us in our pain, and in the process, gives us peace—even as life comes undone!

That peace does not remove the pain of our suffering. Simple answers work only when life is going our way. They fail when life gets complicated and hard. Sometimes God intervenes in clear and miraculous ways. Sometimes the heavens are discouragingly silent. Just as Jesus was not spared the pain of life in a fallen world, nor are we. We will explore the causes of that in the chapters to come.

What *is* promised by Jesus is His presence in our lives—regardless of our circumstances, and it is His presence that is the game changer. One of the many names of God in Scripture is *Emmanuel,* which means "God with us." The fact that God is *with me* in my pain, in my discouragement, in my questioning of Him, in my fatigue, and in my disappointment makes all the difference. I do not face my pain alone. God is with me! God is with you!

Before you close this chapter, go back to the words of Jesus on page 20 and take a moment and think about their implications for your life and for whatever situation you find yourself in. When life comes undone our pain and dislocation is very great. The one constant we have is a God who loves us endlessly, who joins us in our pain, and who never abandons us to it. The landscape of our lives may change forever, but God never changes.

BOLD PRAYER

Father, the dark night of the soul has engulfed my life. You have said that I will face trouble but that I can have peace in You. I ask for that peace right now. You are my hope because You have overcome the world. I believe in the statements You made about Yourself in the book of John, and I claim them for my life. Come into my life, penetrate my pain with your presence and your light. Amen.

QUESTIONS FOR DISCUSSION

What are some moments in your life when life came undone?

Look again at John 16:33. What perspective should this verse give us as we negotiate life? How did Jesus' own life reflect this verse?

As you think about Jesus' statements in the Gospel of John (page 20), how do those truths impact your response when difficulty comes? Which of these truths give you the most comfort?

Have you ever experienced the kind of peace that Jesus refers to? How did that happen and what did it feel like?

CHAPTER TWO

THE UNLIKELY GIFT
Learning to Walk in Faith

Gifts come in different packages. I love gifts—receiving something from someone who loves you, and the mystery of what will be inside the package. But not all gifts are obviously gifts. Some gifts, if we knew what was in them we would never voluntarily unwrap. Life undone is one of these gifts in disguise.

Think about this: *It is a wonderful thing to come to a place where we have nothing to trust in but God.* That is a gift—but a painful and unexpected one.

On Sunday morning January 4, 2008, almost one year after I had left United Hospital in St. Paul after my sojourn of forty-two days, I had just finished a conference in Bangkok, Thailand. It was early morning, and after my 3:00 a.m. wake-up call to get to the airport, I was snuggled into a business-class seat ready for the long trip back to Minneapolis. I dozed as the plane finished loading, the announcements were made, and the plane taxied out to the end of the runway. The last thing I remember was feeling hot and sweating, but I continued to doze.

The next thing I knew, my son Chip was kneeling by my seat, saying "Dad, Dad." A blanket covered me and my vomit. I heard the captain say, "Ladies and gentlemen, we are returning to the gate for a medical emergency," and I groggily asked Chip if that was because of me. He said, "Yes, Dad." I asked what had happened. He said, "You lost consciousness and got sick, and the flight attendant thinks you had a bad seizure. We need to get you to the hospital."

The whole business-class section watched as we were off-loaded through the galley exit to a portable ambulance box lifted up to the plane's galley and then into a regular ambulance. When I was taken off the plane I had no idea what was in store for me. Chip and I were taken to a hospital we knew nothing about. They immediately gave me a brain scan, thinking I had experienced a seizure on the plane. The scan was normal, but the doctor said, "I need to put you in the ICU overnight to watch." I remember asking Chip, "Do you really think that is necessary?"

Arriving at the ICU they put me on monitors and found that my sats were low—not enough oxygen in my blood, and my blood pressure was crashing. An X-ray showed that fluid was quickly building in my lungs and they put me on a machine with a mask that would breathe for me. Chip was frantically explaining to the doctors what had happened a year before when I had MRSA pneumonia and that they needed to give me the full cocktail of antibiotics *now* in case MRSA was back. Using my cell phone he connected them with Mary Ann and my doctors in the states, who confirmed what Chip was telling them.

My sats continued to deteriorate quickly into the afternoon. They decided that they needed to put a central line into my chest that could deliver drugs and fluids rapidly, and measure pressure in the heart. It was *excruciatingly* painful and performed without pain medication. When they could not get the line into my chest, they put it directly into the jugular vein, warning that there was much more, risk but it was necessary.

By late afternoon I had developed massive fluid in both lungs and acute respiratory distress syndrome had set in, along with septic shock. Chip leaned over me as I was struggling to breathe and said "Dad, they need to put you on a ventilator." If there was ever a moment of piercing fear, it was then. The last time I was sick I was on a ventilator for three weeks and should never have survived. Now I am in Thailand, Mary Ann is not here, and my worst fears were being realized. I am in a hospital I don't know, with doctors I don't know, my twenty-one-year-old son is being forced to sign the consent forms, and everything in my mind is screaming, "You won't survive this time."

I asked for a paper and a pen and scratched out the word "Coma?" and the doctor said, "No. We'll put you under for half an hour to intubate you and then you will be awake." And so a few minutes later, I was awake on a ventilator with no control over anything, but I was fully, acutely aware of the fact that I may well not survive even until Mary Ann arrived. It is at times like this that we learn to trust God.

That night was a defining night for me. Not having the benefit of sedation, I knew exactly what was happening and how severe my situation was. Even with the ventilator, my breathing was labored, and each hour they came to suction out the intubation tube, which put my body into convulsions of pain. Facing the reality of my mortality, I had to come to grips with what faith really is. Could I really trust God in this situation? Could I believe in His goodness and love while hovering on the brink of death? Why again? Would I live long enough for Mary Ann to get to Thailand?

The only security I had at that moment, and the long days to come, was the fact that God was with me. And I kept thinking through the words of Jesus to Peter when Peter got out of the boat to walk toward Jesus in the storm: "Take courage! It is I. Don't be afraid" (Mark 6:50). And all I could do was say, "Jesus, I trust you. Whatever happens, I trust You." There was no other place to turn, even if I wanted to. He was the only place I could turn.

Can you identify with a moment like that? When the only place to turn is to God? It is a scary but wonderful thing to come to—a place where we have nothing to trust in but God. It forces us to put our trust in the only place of ultimate hope.

When it is all stripped away, when all of our resources are exhausted as eventually they are, there is the one answer we have had all along: God is there, He is with us, we can trust Him. As Jesus said, "I have told you these things, so that in me you may have peace. In this world you will have trouble. But take heart! I have overcome the world" (John 16:33).

LEARNING TO LIVE BY FAITH

The one common denominator of all great followers of God throughout history is *faith*. Paul reminds us in Romans 1:17, "The righteous will live by faith." What really is faith? First, it is believing that Jesus is the hope of the world as He claimed in the passages in John that we looked at in chapter one. He is the way to the Father. When we say yes to God, acknowledging that Jesus is the Son of God who died for our sins, and we choose to invite Him into our lives, we are putting our faith in Him.

At that moment we become children of God, our hearts are cleaned up, the guilt of our past is lifted, and we have an eternal destiny of life with Christ, forever. The decision to give God the steering wheel of our lives is the most important decision that we will ever make.

In some ways, that is the easy part of faith. The difficult part of the faith walk is learning to trust God for every day, every situation, and every issue that we face. Abraham discovered this, as we all do. Back in the dusty pages of history, God appeared to Abraham with a radical request. "The LORD had said to Abram, 'Leave your country, your people and your father's household and go to the land I will show you'" (Genesis 12:1).

Now Abraham could not Google the new location to see what it looked like, he had no map to follow, and no knowledge of what God had in store for him. What he had was faith in God as God, so he chose to take his family and start a life journey based on faith. That is why Abraham is the great example and hero of faith for Jesus and Paul in the New Testament.

Take a moment and put yourself in Abraham's shoes. I doubt that he was initially overjoyed at God's request. You want me to do what? You want me to go where? Why? Why me? I'll bet that Abraham spent months sitting in his tent asking himself a set of questions:

- Do I really trust God?
- Do I believe that God has my best interests in mind?
- Am I willing to trust Him with my future? Really trust Him?
- Am I willing to take the risk of following God?

Faith is scary and risky! Faith means that I am saying to God, "I am all in. I trust You fully, I believe You have my very best interests in mind, I am willing to trust You with my future, and I am willing to take the risk to follow You. I even believe that Your plan for my life has eternal purposes that are beyond my understanding but give great glory to You."

Life undone is an unlikely gift. It invites us to take a giant step of faith that we have never before taken, to a depth we have never before gone, because we have come to the end of ourselves and have no other good choices. Life undone invites us to answer the question, "Are we all in with God, and can we trust Him with our future?"

Lying in my hospital bed in Thailand, hooked up to five or six drip lines, a feeding tube, the ventilator breathing for me, staring at a blank wall and a clock, left only with my thoughts, I had to ask the same questions as Abraham. Do I really believe? Can I really trust? Is God really with me? Can He give me peace in the midst of my undone life and tenuous health? Is He enough if He is all I have?

In my heart I knew the answer, and said, "Yes." God, who had been so faithful in my life for so long, was not going to abandon His goodness and faithfulness and presence now. And then it came to me: In that moment I realized that I had just been given a great gift. I had nowhere to turn but to God, and now I had the opportunity to trust Him completely. I was all in—no matter what the outcome. It was an hour-by-hour faith, as times of trouble are—and yes, I experienced that peace that only Jesus gives because I had reaffirmed that I would live by faith and trust Him unconditionally.

Faith is easy when life is good. Faith is tested and hard when life is undone, because now we must grapple with the *goodness of God* in addition to the *plan of God*. We may even face moments of doubt (Is my faith well-founded?) or anger (Why would God allow this?) or resignation (Is God really in my corner?).

These are legitimate, important, and good questions because they force us back to God in prayer, force us back to His Word, and again confront us with the reality of following Him. Every time we choose to answer the big questions in the affirmative, our faith is strengthened and God is glorified. This faith is based now on a higher level of conviction than before because our faith has been chosen in pain and difficulty.

STEPPING STONES OF HARD FAITH

Faith does not happen overnight. Learning faith is like learning to walk as a toddler. We finally pull ourselves up and wobble around, fall on our face, pull ourselves up again, and finally make it across the room into the hands of our parents.

When God called Abraham, He did not tell him all that was in store for him. He asked him to take a step of faith and follow Him. As Abraham did that, his faith grew and he was able to take a greater step of faith.

When life comes undone and we are inundated with pain, faith is a moment-by-moment and day-by-day challenge. Sometimes just making it through the next hour or the next night trusting God is all that we can do.

Every hour lying in my ICU bed in Thailand, awake on a ventilator, was like living through twenty-four hours. What sustained me was not some grand faith for my future, but trust in God to help me get through the next *hour,* and the next day. I *clung* like the dying man I was to the promise that God was with me, and prayed for the peace of His presence. Time and again I had to remind myself of His promises and ask Him for His peace. It was a battle of faith that I had never experienced before.

Physical or emotional pain drives us either to deeper faith or away from faith to disillusionment. Pain is debilitating. The question is whether we will *choose* to take that first step of faith even though our reserves are low, we feel alone, fear is high, and we find it hard to understand where God figures in the equation. A small step toward God allows us to take the next, which allows us to take the next, but it is *one* step at a time of hard trust in the face of deep emotional challenge. It is a hard faith—but hard faith is the most real faith because we choose to believe and trust when belief and trust is at its most difficult.

Hard faith is the decision that we will trust and follow Jesus, regardless of our circumstances, believing that He is good and righteous and holy and has a plan for our lives that is beyond our understanding. The writer to the Hebrews wrote, "Now faith is being sure of what we hope for and certain of what we do not see" (Hebrews 11:1). Further, "without faith it is impossible to please God, because anyone who comes to him must believe that he exists and that he rewards those who earnestly seek him" (Hebrews 11:6).

And then referencing Abraham, the writer said, "By faith Abraham, when called to go to a place he would later receive as his inheritance, obeyed and went, even though he did not know where he was going" (Hebrews 11:8).

When life comes undone, we face Abraham moments. Will we believe, will we trust, will we follow? In the face of not understanding, will we take that small step of hard faith toward God? You may be facing one of those moments right now. Your choice will make all the difference in the world as to how you walk out the difficulties you face. Faith is always a choice. What is your choice?

Countless times in Hebrews 11 we read the two words "By faith", at the beginning of a verse, about an individual who chose to follow God when all the chips were down. They include Abel, Enoch, Noah, Abraham, Isaac, Jacob, Joseph, Moses, Rahab, Gideon, Barak, Samson, Jepthah, David, and numerous others. The common trait in each of these men and women of God was their choice of faith not only in the good times but in the hard and difficult times. Because of their faith they show up on God's hall of fame in the great chapter of faith in Hebrews 11.

That hall of fame continues to grow. Every time we choose faith over doubt, despair, or anger, we join those whose names are listed above. Remember, God "rewards those who earnestly seek him." He rewards those who *choose* Him, those who trust Him!

Faith is directly connected to the peace that Jesus promised in John 16:33: "I have told you these things, so that in me you may have peace. In this world you will have trouble. But take heart! I have overcome the world."

Where does that peace come from that Jesus talks about? He says, "In me" you may have peace. In Me! Our peace is not in our circumstances (they can be very bad). It is not in our conviction that everything will go back to the way it was before (it may well not). It is not in our ability to solve our problem (we may not be able to). No, our peace comes from our trust in the person of Jesus Christ. We can have peace *in Him,* in His presence, in His goodness, in His love, in His promise to be with us, and in His power to overcome the world.

When it is all stripped away, when all of our resources are exhausted, as eventually they are, there is the one answer we have had all along: God is there, He is with us, we can trust Him. Do you today? Are you willing to give your situation to God in faith with a simple childlike trust and say, "Jesus, I am all in. I trust You with my pain, and like Abraham, I will follow not knowing where I am going. One small step at a time."

FAITH AS A JOURNEY, NOT A DESTINATION

The challenge of faith is that we cannot see where it will end. My metaphor for faith is a hike that I have taken many times near Big Sky, Montana, at Lava Lake. It is a long, steep hike that requires me to stop for rests on a regular basis. You cannot see very far ahead, just to the next bend in the trail, so you set your mind on that next bend, knowing that at least you can stop and rest when you get there. But then there is another bend and another. It is not unusual to see hikers tending to blisters and tired feet as the ascent is steep and difficult. It is a narrow, dusty trail scattered with sharp protruding rocks and littered with loose stones. Many ankles have been turned and legs bruised on this trail.

Life is a journey of faith in Jesus. He gives us what we need to see to the next bend but not around it. Each time we reach the bend, we must again renew our faith for the next section of the trail, following, trusting, believing, and continuing. What strengthens us along the way are the fellow travelers who are also trusting God—and the fact that God has proved to be faithful in the past so we can trust Him to remain faithful in the future.

Sometimes on the Lava Lake trail you turn the bend and you just see another steep climb. Other times you come across cool shade beside a mountain stream where you can stop, relax, and recharge. That is the nature of trails—it is the nature of pilgrimage—it is the nature of faith. One step at a time!

As I look back on my life I am glad that I could not see beyond the next bend in the road, because I would not have had the strength to go there if I knew what was in front of me. Some bends have been exhilarating and challenging and joyful. Others have required hard faith, the courage to keep going, and the need to trust God in ways that I had never trusted before.

In each instance, however, God has been faithful and has provided what I needed at the moment. As Jesus said, "I have told you these things, so that in me you may have peace. In this world you will have trouble. But take heart! I have overcome the world" (John 16:33).

The apostle Paul faced an amazing series of challenges in his ministry, including death threats, beatings, illness, shipwrecks, deep opposition, riots, mistrust of others, times of deep poverty, and the list could go on. He, too, learned that God was sufficient for what he needed at any given moment, in spite of his current circumstances.

> For I have learned to be content whatever the circumstances. I know what it is to be in need, and I know what it is to have plenty. I have learned the secret of being content in any and every situation, whether well fed or hungry, whether living in plenty or in want. I can do everything through him who gives me strength. (Philippians 4:11-13)

The secret? God gives us the strength we need, when we need it, to get to the next bend in the trail, whatever the trail we are walking. For me in the Thailand ICU, that was often the strength to get through the next hour, to endure the next suctioning of the vent into my chest, to get through the long, hard nights without sleep and in great pain, wondering if the morning X-ray would show progress, deeper problems, or just more of the discouraging same.

We often look at those going through deep valleys and wonder, *how do they do it?* Here is the answer: When we face tough times, God gives us exactly what we need to meet *those* circumstances. He may not give us more than we need, but He will not give us less than we need. His presence and His strength match the challenge we face. Our part is to place our trust and faith in Him and boldly ask Him for what we need.

Sometimes what we think we need is not really what we need! Early on in the Thailand ICU, I pleaded with God to take the pain away. He didn't. And I finally asked myself, "Why should He? He, after all endured amazing pain yet continued to trust His father." So I then asked Him to give me the strength to endure the pain and His presence to grant me peace. And that He did. That is what I really needed!

I first met Erik when he was about five years old, a blond-haired, precocious little boy. I was his pastor in a new church in California. Eventually his parents left their job, feeling called to seminary and then ministry. Years later I received devastating news: Erik, now seventeen, was missing in Colorado. A desperate search ensued only to find Erik's lifeless body in his car where he had committed suicide, his Bible open next to him.

A series of events and deep depression had led Erik to an unthinkable act in a dark night of the soul. He left two sisters, parents, and many friends devastated from wounds that never completely heal.

For his parents, my friends Dennis and Pauline, the pain was numbing and gut-wrenching. Like Abraham they had left everything to follow God into ministry, and some of those very moves contributed, it would seem, to Erik's troubles. The "why" questions rocked their soul! The strength to get through another day took everything they had. In addition, this took place as they were in job transition, so everything in their lives was in upheaval.

Dennis was the elder who dedicated my own son, Jon, a few years younger than his son. Every time he saw Jon, he was reminded of the loss he lived with each day. How did they make it through? They climbed a steep, hard trail of faith, trusting God to get them to the next bend, and the next, and the next, till one day it became easier, and then easier as God put together what had been life undone. God gave them what they needed in the moment, for each day, and continues to do so when the loss of their precious son brings a new wave of grief, many years later.

When I entered the hospital in Thailand, my wife, Mary Ann, was nine thousand miles away in Minnesota. She got a call about 9:00 p.m. that I had just been taken off the plane. By 3:00 p.m. the next day she was on a plane and a twenty-four-hour trip to Bangkok. For nearly three days I was without her presence, desperately wanting her to arrive. Hoping I would survive until she arrived. When she got there, everything changed. I was not any better; in fact, I was still heading the wrong direction, but she was there and it was a comfort.

In the same way, God's presence in our pain is a "game changer." Our situation is still painful, we still wrestle with the undoneness of our lives, but He is there, He is present, and He gives us what we need in the moment till we reach the next bend—not knowing what is there, but knowing that His presence will sustain us to the next place. He was there for Abraham, He was there for Dennis and Pauline, He was there for Mary Ann and me. He is there right now for you.

It is a wonderful thing to come to the place where all we have to trust in is God. In the end that is all that we need. And in the pain of life having come undone, the presence and provision of God is an unlikely but very real gift. It is like the payoff when one reaches the top of the Lava Lake climb. There you break out of the trees to the sight of a high pristine mountain lake with a beautiful craggy rock shoreline. It is a place of beauty, rest, quiet, and peace. That is what the presence of God brings to tired souls who are struggling along the path of life undone.

BOLD PRAYER

Father, yes, I am all in. I choose to trust You with my circumstance and my pain. Like Abraham, I will follow You wherever the path leads; I don't know where it goes, but You do. I choose faith and I choose to walk with You in the hard times as well as the good times. Be with me and give me Your peace, because it is in You that peace is found. I thank You that You have overcome the world. Amen.

QUESTIONS FOR DISCUSSION

Have you ever had an Abraham moment when God asked you to step out in faith without knowing what the outcome would be? What was that like and how did it mold you?

Read Hebrews 11. What stands out to you about the faith of those listed in this chapter? How does the writer of Hebrews 11 specifically commend those who chose faith over other options?

How would you characterize what walking in faith really is from Hebrews 11?

Share your own struggles in choosing faith over doubt, anger, and despair in a circumstance in your life.

CHAPTER THREE

DIVINE SCARS
The Fellowship of His Sufferings

When life comes undone it leaves painful scars. We deal with emotional pain, physical trauma, limitations, and life issues that are impacted by our situation. Often it is all followed by a long period of rebuilding physically, emotionally, financially, and in ways that we never could have imagined. All of this can come as a shock to someone who has never before faced such challenges. Lives that were good and normal and joyful, suddenly are invaded by pain, the abnormal, and unmitigated stress.

Instinctively we ask one question: *Why? Why me?*

The "why?" question makes me think of Joseph in the Old Testament. He was the favorite son of his father (remember the coat of many colors?). In jealousy his brothers sold him to a passing caravan as a slave. Don't you think Joseph, who was most likely a teenager, was asking, why me? He ends up in the home of a high official and demonstrates his skill and trustworthiness to the point that his master gives him full control of his household. But his master's wife has eyes for him, and when he refuses her advances, she claims he tried to rape her. He is thrown into jail for years. Again, I can imagine him asking, why? He has been faithful to his God and his master and this is what he gets in return!

As I said, it is a wonderful thing to come to the place where we have no one to turn to but God. That is where Joseph found himself as he languished in jail for doing the right thing. He was experiencing the dark night of the soul, his life had come undone for the second time— first slavery and then this, but in pain he discovered the goodness and presence of God.

> But while Joseph was there in the prison, the LORD was with him; he showed him kindness and granted him favor in the eyes of the prison warden. So the warden put Joseph in charge of all those held in the prison, and he was made responsible for all that was done there. The warden paid no attention to anything under Joseph's care, because the LORD was with Joseph and gave him success in whatever he did. (Genesis 39:20-23)

After years went by, two important prisoners showed up in prison with Joseph, the king's cupbearer and baker. One would not think such positions to be that important, but in that day, these guys were literally the "secret service" because they had intimate proximity to the king, provided the king's food, and actually sampled it themselves first to ensure that it was not poisoned. They were as close to the king as anyone in the palace. They were his intelligence network to what was happening in the palace and beyond.

Both the cupbearer and baker had a dream while in prison, and no one could interpret the dream except Joseph, whom God gave divine insight. He accurately told the baker that he would be executed and the cupbearer that he would be freed. He asked the cupbearer to remember him when he got out, since he was a man of influence and could have sprung Joseph from prison.

Instead, the cupbearer promptly forgot Joseph, and another two years passed in prison. What do you suppose was going through Joseph's mind during those long interminable years in a dank, dirty, smelly, ancient prison?

One thing Joseph had to conclude: Life is not fair, people are not fair, and circumstances are not fair. It does not take long in life to realize all three of these things to be true. All one needs to do is watch the news to know that life is not fair and injustice is common. Probably everyone reading this book has experienced personal injustice and unfairness. Many workplaces provide ample opportunity, as well as friends who betray us, or even fellow believers who are malicious and cruel.

But God had not forgotten Joseph, and one day it was Pharaoh who had a dream that none of his advisors could interpret. Now the cupbearer suddenly remembered the prisoner who had accurately interpreted his dream, and he told Pharaoh about Joseph. So Joseph was brought before Pharaoh, and he shared with the king that God had ordained seven years of plenty for Egypt to be followed by seven years of famine. He counseled Pharaoh to find a wise and diligent individual to store up food during the seven years of plenty so that the nation would not starve during the seven years of famine. Recognizing that the Spirit of God was on Joseph, Pharaoh made Joseph the second in command in Egypt to oversee the storing and distribution of food.

As he had predicted to Pharaoh, there were seven years of great harvests and then seven years of famine. Joseph had led the effort to store food for the day of famine, and one day his brothers came from their homeland to purchase food from Egypt as all the surrounding countries were forced to do. Imagine the scene when the brothers, who had sold Joseph into slavery, stood before him, now a high official of Pharaoh, not knowing who they were depending on to purchase food for their family.

Never was there a better opportunity for Joseph to get revenge, but Joseph understood that God had a purpose in his suffering—that what his brothers meant for evil, God redeemed and used for good—as God always does if we will let Him.

> Then Joseph said to his brothers, "Come close to me." When they had done so, he said, "I am your brother Joseph, the one you sold into Egypt! And now, do not be distressed and do not be angry with yourselves for selling me here, because it was to save lives that God sent me ahead of you. For two years now there has been famine in the land, and for the next five years there will not be plowing and reaping. But God sent me ahead of you to preserve for you a remnant on earth and to save your lives by a great deliverance. (Genesis 45:4-7)

Joseph realized that God could take the unfairness, the evil actions of his brothers, the pain of false accusations, imprisonment, and slavery and use them for His good and eternal purposes. When life came undone, he could not see that. In light of the years that had passed, he now had a perspective that was far different.

REDEEMING PAIN FOR LARGER PURPOSES

During the times of crisis and pain, there are days when the goal is simply to make it through the day. Just surviving another physically or emotionally exhausting day is victory.

What is not evident in the moment is that God is at work redeeming our pain for His glory. As I look back over my life, I realize that it was in the difficult times, when life had come undone, that I experienced the most profound periods of growth. When life is good, pleasant, and wonderful, we often don't see a lot of personal growth. But when life is hard, painful, or challenging, we are forced toward God and faith in Him, rather than our own resources. In fact, every major spiritual advance I have had has been in the context of life coming undone!

Peter reminded his readers of this truth in 1 Peter 1:6-7:

> In this you greatly rejoice, though now for a little while
> you may have had to suffer grief in all kinds of trials.
> These have come so that your faith—of greater worth
> than gold, which perishes even though refined by fire—
> may be proved genuine and may result in praise, glory
> and honor when Jesus Christ is revealed.

God's greatest goal for our lives is not to make us happy and content. His greatest goal is to help us become like Him in character and heart. It is in the hard times that we actually develop the faith that brings us true joy in life. Thus our pain, from whatever direction it comes, gives us the gift of turning our hearts in need to the only one who can truly satisfy our hearts: Christ. In the moment, all we may feel is pain. In the scope of life, if we turn to Him, that pain develops in us deep faith and character that looks like His character.

The first time life came undone for us it was early in my career when the church I was serving encountered problems, forcing me to take a different path. I chose to resign and move from California back to Minnesota to figure out what to do next. It had been a dark night of the soul, and I was physically exhausted, emotionally wounded, and deeply clinically depressed. From my perspective at the time, my dreams were shattered, we had been mistreated, and I no longer wanted to continue as a pastor. The trajectory of my life had taken a 180 degree turn, and like an errant missile, exploded.

It was a painful and long recovery that took a full ten years. But it launched me on a journey to understand God's grace in my life—a journey that continues to this day. Redeeming my painful experience in that church, God gave me a consulting and writing career to help church leadership become healthy and effective. As with Joseph, God took what was ugly and painful and full of despair and redeemed it for His purposes, and in the process grew my heart more like His heart.

As God uses our pain to help us become like Him in character and heart, we actually find ourselves becoming content and happy. The route to that contentment and happiness is not the one we would choose, because it runs through the river of pain, but it emerges on the other side with an authentic contentment and happiness that we couldn't have by any other means. And in the process we begin to understand the promise of Jesus: "I have come that they may have life, and have it to the full" (John 10:10).

I meet many people whose ministries were born out of pain in their own lives. Karen, for instance, early in her life chose to terminate a pregnancy, and for years she lived with the guilt and sorrow of that decision. That pain and God's healing grace led her to help other women who live with the same painful secret to find healing and freedom (www. GoDeeperStill.org).

Another friend was profoundly wounded when his twin brother, his only sibling, was killed at twenty years old in a helicopter accident. A local business was giving rides as a promotion, and the chopper went down killing his brother and fiancée. Any sibling can be hard to lose but an inseparable twin is especially hard.

The pain of that loss led my friend to devote his life to helping evangelistic efforts around the world. His brother had not known Christ, and God used the pain and his subsequent encounter with Jesus to fund ministries of evangelism. He set out to do all he could to ensure that as many as possible hear the Good News and have a chance to say yes to God. Again, God took pain and redeemed it for His higher purposes.

Here is what you need to know if life has come undone. God is not the author of your pain—pain comes from living in a broken world. But God will take your pain and redeem it for His greater eternal purposes if you will allow Him to do that. The route to true fulfillment and purpose is often found in a detour through unwelcome pain. Just as He did with Joseph, God wants to take that pain and use it for His glory. He will use our suffering to build His character and heart in us more fully.

CHOOSING DIVINE SCARS

When life comes undone, when we face a Joseph moment, we are tempted to respond in different ways:

- Anger: Why would God allow this to happen to me? I don't deserve this.
- Denial: I will just ignore this and it will go away. These are people who don't live in reality or deal with their pain.
- Depression: I can't handle this and I allow myself to sink into despair.
- Retribution: I am going to get the person who did this to me. Think of a spouse that has been abandoned for another person.

None of these responses, while deeply human, lead us to a healthy place. We do not control life's circumstances, but each of us has a choice as to how we respond to them. There is a better choice and one that God wants us to choose: to simply trust Him in whatever pain we face. To join God's hall of fame of faith in Hebrews 11.

All of us have scars from life. I don't want just scars, I want divine scars. Divine scars come from times when life comes undone—when hurt, tragedy, pain, unfairness, sorrow, and difficulty come into our lives—and we allow God to change our hearts in the process. They come when we choose to trust Him in our loss rather than turn to bitterness or despair. They are scars that have been redeemed for a higher eternal purpose.

I am fascinated that when Jesus rose from the dead, He rose with a new body, but still a human body, and He still bore the scars in His hands and feet. In fact, Jesus chose to identify with us as humans from the point of His incarnation, and when we see Him in heaven, we will see Him in human form with the scars.

Those scars are divine scars. They represent His death and resurrection for us. They represent His willingness to follow even when it was hard. His ultimate test came on the Thursday evening prior to his death when, through intense struggle, He chose to say "YES" to the father in those faithful words, "My Father, if it is not possible for this cup to be taken away unless I drink it, may your will be done" (Matthew 26:42).

Many forget that Christ suffered not only in His death but in His life. Seven hundred years before His birth, the prophet Isaiah accurately described Christ in these terms: "He was despised and rejected by men, a man of sorrows and familiar with suffering" (Isaiah 53:3).

Think about the words "despised," "rejected," "sorrows," and "suffering." These words were the reality for much of Jesus' life and ministry. His life was a life of choosing to follow His Father, and that following included suffering and hard times.

Jesus also told His disciples that their life of following Him would be like His following His Father, and that it, too, would include hardships. "Anyone who does not take his cross and follow me is not worthy of me. Whoever finds his life will lose it, and whoever loses his life for my sake will find it" (Matthew 10:38-39). The cross we are to take up is like the cross of Jesus—a symbol of suffering. And following Him will mean losing our lives for His sake: Giving our lives to Him for His purposes, rather than pursuing our own.

This brings us back to the principle that God's greatest goal for our lives is not to make us happy and content. His greatest goal is to help us become like Him in character and heart. This will mean times of sorrow and suffering, just as He faced sorrow and suffering. In fact, it is precisely in those times of hardship that He has the greatest opportunity to mold our hearts, character, priorities, and commitments.

And what happens when we suffer while following Jesus? When we choose to trust when the chips are down? When we experience sorrow as He experienced it?

Paul puts it this way in his own life: "I want to know Christ and the power of his resurrection and the fellowship of sharing in his sufferings, becoming like him in his death, and so, somehow, to attain to the resurrection from the dead" (Philippians 3:10-11).

The phrase "fellowship of sharing in his sufferings" is an amazing phrase for anyone whose life has come undone. As Christ followers, when we suffer, we simply share in the suffering of Christ Himself. When I laid in the hospital bed in Thailand, wondering whether I would live or die, I was sharing in the sufferings of Christ. When my friend Doug was wasting away from ALS, one indignity at a time, he was sharing in the sufferings of Christ. When my friend Marge's husband walked out on her never to return, she shared in the sufferings of Christ. As Josh gets used to his wheelchair, he is sharing in the suffering of Christ. As Dennis and Pauline mourn the loss of their son, Eric, they share in the fellowship of Christ's sufferings. When Jim and Megan buried their precious stillborn daughter, Karanaugh, they shared in the fellowship of Christ's sufferings.

When we join Christ in His work, we also join *Him* in the sorrows, grief, and suffering. No longer am I experiencing sorrow, grief, and suffering by myself and without purpose. Now I do it in fellowship with Jesus—with Him and for Him. In the process, we are profoundly changed and become more like Him!

Even the suffering Jesus experienced had a higher purpose. Again, the writer of Hebrews says this about Christ:

> During the days of Jesus' life on earth, he offered up prayers and petitions with loud cries and tears to the one who could save him from death, and he was heard

because of his reverent submission. Although he was
a son, he learned obedience from what he suffered.
(Hebrews 5:7-8)

We are not the only ones who come to the end of ourselves and find
that all we have to turn to is God. That was true for Jesus when He
walked our earth. But notice that it says He, like us, learned obedience
from what He suffered. His suffering, like ours, had a higher eternal
purpose that God was using to mold and shape Him—even though He
was the Son of God and perfect. I don't want to suffer for the sake of
suffering, but if in my suffering I share in the fellowship of Christ's suffering, and if He uses it for higher eternal purposes in my life, then I am
willing to accept suffering and sorrow as part of the equation of following Jesus in a broken world. Now I have a divine purpose infused into
my suffering, along with the presence of Christ in the midst of suffering.

At age fifty-five, I have a lot of scars. I call them divine scars because
they are scars that God has used to change me, grow me, mold me,
change my heart, and deepen my faith. Here are some of the sources of
my divine scars:

- People who have treated me poorly
- Significant illness
- Being misunderstood
- Forced out of a job
- Being unemployed
- Financial difficulties
- Slander and gossip
- Family challenges
- Marriage stresses
- Discouragements
- Church disillusionment

Just as I have physical scars from two long stays in the hospital, I
also have emotional and relational scars. God has used them to grow me
and change me and teach me in my journey of faith. I have shared in

the fellowship of His sufferings. You have too! Just as Jesus will wear His scars in heaven, so will we. And we will understand then what is hard to understand now: God had purposes in our lives that we did not know. We will see that our suffering contributed in some way to our growth and faith, and it all had a place in His eternal divine drama in our world. I look forward, as I am sure you do, to seeing how all the pieces come together. One day they will.

GOD'S GRACE IN THE PROCESS

When I was awake on the ventilator in Thailand, I could not talk, so I had to write notes to family and doctors. Six of those notes stand out:

The worst day I can remember in my life

I have to get extubated, I can't take it anymore

This is where coma or heaven sounds nice

I am very weary

I just want to sleep

Coma?

I cannot explain the difficulty breathing, the pain I experienced, and the excruciating nature of the hourly suctioning of the intubation tube. I have said it was like eleven days of waterboarding and every hour felt like a day. To put off the suctioning I would wait as long as I could, but fluid would gather in the bottom of the tube so that it felt like I was drowning or breathing through mud. To call for suctioning meant enduring the pain of that procedure. It was a no-win situation.

As I have read the statements I wrote to my family and doctors, I think it is the way many feel when life comes undone. How long can I take this? Massive weariness! Hard, terrible, painful days! But what I learned, and what we all learn, is that God's grace and presence is sufficient to see us through—even when we face the worst suffering possible.

During the worst hours, I kept running the words of Jesus to Peter through my mind, "Take courage! It is I. Don't be afraid" (Matthew 14:27). God did not give me what I needed for the next day or the next week, but He did give me what I needed for that hour and that day. It came back to the promise of Jesus: "In me you may have peace" (John 16:33). All I had was Jesus, and He was enough.

I don't know your situation. Life comes undone is so many ways. What I do know is that God will give you what you need today, in this hour, in this moment, and will continue to do so as you walk your unique journey. There are scars but they are divine scars that will change you in ways you cannot imagine. And you are sharing in the fellowship of His sufferings. Allow this amazing fact to encourage you and give you hope: If you are sharing in His sufferings, you are also sharing in His presence for this is a *fellowship* of His sufferings.

I am proud of the divine scars I wear today. They are the result of following Jesus when the chips were down, of forging faith in the hard times, of learning to take the next step and walk to the next bend, and trusting God in the present. Divine scars are worthy scars. They change us. They make our hearts more like the heart of Jesus. Wear your divine scars with pride. They are proof of your faith forged in the realities of everyday life—and even of life undone.

BOLD PRAYER

Father, there are times when I am weary and wonder if I can go on. I ask You to be what You need for me in this moment. Transform my scars into divine scars that will mold and change me and honor You. I rejoice that my suffering is not without purpose, and that in my suffering, I share in the fellowship of Your sufferings. Like Joseph, help me to see Your greater purposes in what I am walking through.

QUESTIONS FOR DISCUSSION

What can we learn from Joseph's story about suffering and God's greater purposes for our lives and His work?

How does the suffering Jesus experienced (see Isaiah 53; Hebrews 5) help us put our suffering into perspective?

Why do you think so many believers think they should be immune from hardship and suffering?

What perspective on suffering does Romans 5:1-6 give us?

Share some of the divine scars you have and how God has used those scars in your life and spiritual growth.

CREATION INTERRUPTED
Why Bad Things Happen

Years ago there was a popular book titled *When Bad Things Happen to Good People*. The reason it was popular is that it attempted to answer the age-old question of why we must endure suffering in this world. This question has been asked since the beginning of time and is the subject of a whole book in the Old Testament—the book of Job.

We all ask this question at one time or another when life comes undone; when bad things happen that are beyond our control; when the tsunami of sorrow, pain, and dislocation engulfs our lives. Why does a loving God allow pain? Where is God in the injustices we see all around us? Why does God not always answer our fervent prayers and deepest hopes? Why must I live with divine scars?

We are inundated with all kinds of spiritual sophistry that would have us believe that pain does not need to come our way; that faith will cure all; that God meant for us to live in perpetual happiness, health, and financial prosperity. Yet we know that is not true in our lives. We also know that this is not what Scripture promises. As Jesus said, "I have told you these things, so that in me you may have peace. In this world you will have trouble But take heart! I have overcome the world" (John 16:33).

What do I say when I look into Dennis and Pauline's eyes after they lost their wonderful son to suicide? I had been Eric's pastor years before when he was a happy, precocious little boy. Now in the midst of depression he has taken his life, his open Bible next to him. He knew Jesus, he desperately wanted to please Him, yet the dark night of the soul overwhelmed him for reasons we don't understand, and now Dennis and Pauline have only memories and a gravesite. The scar of losing a child never leaves a parent. It is not supposed to be this way. Why?

What do I say to those who lost a loved one in an accident or after a long illness when God chose to spare my life? They prayed just as hard and fervently for the miracle that twice became mine, but it did not become theirs. Why?

I am sure you have asked the question, why? in your own life journey. We know God is good and that He is able, but life comes undone in so many painful ways and we ask why—even when we choose to trust in God's ultimate goodness.

Is there an answer to the question why?

To answer that question we need to go back to the beginning of the story of this planet and God's creation of an amazing, perfect, peaceful, sinless, and harmonious world.

In the beginning, when God created the heavens and the earth, it was with His word that God created light, the sky, the land, the flora, the sun and moon and stars, the creatures of the sea, and the creatures of the land:

> Then God said, "Let us make man in our image, in our
> likeness, and let them rule over the fish of the sea and
> the birds of the air, over the livestock, over all the earth,
> and over all the creatures that move along the ground."
> So God created man in his own image, in the image of
> God he created him; male and female he created them.
> . . . God saw all that he had made, and it was very good.
> (Genesis 1:26-27,31)

When God says it was very good, it must have been very, very good. It was a place of peace, joy, relational closeness between Adam and Eve, the creation, and God. None of the scars that mar our lives, our workplaces, or our globe were present. It was very good.

A WORLD UNDONE

In contrast to that perfect, peaceful, sinless, and good creation, think with me about some of the descriptors of today's world. Grinding poverty, conflict, hopelessness, selfishness, war, corruption, abortion, guilt, shame, natural disasters, global economic collapse, death, disease, human trafficking, sexual slavery, infidelity, drugs, sorrow, materialism, murder, rape, torture, kidnapping, injustice, pollution, terrorism, family breakdown, tears, jealousy, envy, anger, hatred, selfishness, and the list could go on.

Something has gone *terribly* wrong. When Adam and Eve chose to disobey God and follow the advice of Satan, God's great adversary, the perfect creation literally came undone, and we have been living with the consequences of that unraveling since. Perfection became imperfection. Joy was replaced by pain. Eternal beings become mortal and subject to disease and death. Hearts that were one with God became estranged from God, and subject to all the sinful and dark urges of men and women no longer in communion with the One who created them. So great was the dislocation and shift caused by sin that it is hard for us to get our minds around that cosmic earthquake that changed everything.

This is all the more tragic because God thought so much of those He created, that He created us in His image. He fashioned us in ways that were consistent with His own character: He gave us pure hearts that could connect with His, a moral nature that could distinguish right from wrong, the ability to rule over creation as He ruled over all of the created order, the ability to be creative and solve problems.

That, too, all changed when Adam and Eve chose to follow Satan rather than God. While we're still created in His image, that image has become dulled, and the connection between God and man was broken. No longer did we have God's heart or character. Now our lives were under the influence of sin and evil and Satan.

The tragedy of this fallen and broken world is evident in the pain we see around us. Eric's death and suicide is a symptom of a broken world that also breaks people. Life comes undone precisely because the world has come undone through sin and the influence of the evil one, Satan. If you wonder if Satan exists, all you need to do is watch the nightly news with its preponderance of bad news, or think of the situations that wake you up at night in concern or prayer. This is not the world God created, and that is the great cosmic tragedy.

It is easy to blame God for bad things that happen in this world. The truth is that in blaming Him we are doing something even more terrible: We are blaming the perfect and holy God who created a perfect and holy creation for the sin that we as humans brought into the world in rebellion against Him. In essence, He created a perfect world, but we rebelled and now blame Him for the imperfect world. We ask why He allows bad things to happen, why He tolerates injustice and evil and sorrow and pain. Blame is heaped on the very One whose character is holy and good and righteous, the One who sought the very best for men and women made in His image who instead chose to rebel and go their own way. That is the greatest possible transfer of responsibility ever!

With that kind of response to God's goodness and that trashing of what was good and holy and right, what would you have done if you were God? I would have walked away! Forever! Leaving our sorry planet and ungrateful people to the consequences of their choices and the folly of their ways. Fortunately, He did not do that. Instead, He instantly initiated a rescue operation to redeem what had been so good and had now gone so bad.

THE THIEF AND THE GOOD SHEPHERD

Jesus put this divine drama into perspective in John 10:10 where he told his disciples, "The thief comes only to steal and kill and destroy; I have come that they may have life and have it to the full."

Why does Jesus call Satan a thief? Because from the beginning of time, it has been his strategy and intention to *steal* the good that God fashioned in creation and to substitute a fake in its place that cannot satisfy and that destroys rather than heals.

When Jesus says that the thief comes only to steal and kill and destroy, He is accurately defining the intentions of the evil one for our world and for you and me. Satan is a destroyer of all that is good. His ultimate goal is to remove us from the goodness of God, to devalue life, to wreck what it means to be made in God's image, and to substitute a cheap imitation of his own for real life with God.

When I travel to certain parts of Asia, I am accosted on the street by men saying, "Copy watch, copy watch, copy watch." They want to sell me a cheap imitation of a Rolex or other high-caliber watch that is a fake and will last maybe till I get off the plane back home. That is the strategy of Satan. He wants to sell us a cheap imitation of the real thing that will hurt and destroy rather than build and heal.

Thus he tries to sell us on the fact that accumulation of wealth will bring happiness, which it does not. He tries to sell us on a lie that unlimited sex and sensual pleasures outside of a monogamous marriage relationship will bring satisfaction, when it does not. He tries to sell us on the lie that all paths lead to God, which only results in many people who will never find God. He tries to sell us on doing what we need to do to get ahead even when it hurts and devalues people, which is one of his ultimate goals.

Satan is a fraud, a liar, a destroyer, a thief, a killer, and a peddler of fraudulent truth. That is why the world is undone and why it continues to be undone. Contrast that with the Good Shepherd: "I have come that they [you] may have life, and have it to the full" (John 10:10).

Satan brings death. Jesus brings life. When Jesus talks about life, He is talking about all those things connected to life. Here are some of the elements that Jesus includes when He says He brings life:

- The forgiveness of my sin (John 3:16)
- The removal of my guilt (Romans 8:1-2)
- The ongoing presence of His Holy Spirit in my life (Ephesians 1:13-14)
- The ability to choose good over evil (James 4:7-8)
- A change in my personal priorities (Romans 12:1-2)
- A purpose and passion for life (Ephesians 2:10)
- The fruit of His Spirit in my life (Galatians 5:22-26)
- The healing of wounds of life and of sin (Romans 5:1-8)
- Justice and mercy in our world (Micah 6:8)
- Care for the widow, orphan, hungry, and hurting (Isaiah 58)
- Relational unity and loving relationships (1 John)
- A world infected by His righteousness (Matthew 5–7)

To emphasize His point Jesus said that He came that we may have life, and have it to the full! He came so that our lives could overflow with all the good things of God compared to the destruction, pain, sorrow, and fakery of the evil one.

The thief is intent on destroying everything good while the Good Shepherd is intent on destroying everything bad and redeeming that which has been made bad by sin and the influence of the evil one. As we will see, there is no doubt who will win this divine drama. In the meantime we live in a war zone between the forces of good and the forces of evil. And we are members of God's redemption army, playing a crucial role in the battle.

Many wonder if God has an A and B plan for our lives. Jesus said He has one plan for our lives: that we might have life and it to the full. In a great irony, Jesus takes even the pain in our lives and uses that pain to bring us ultimate joy—if we allow Him to. What the thief tries to steal, Jesus loves to redeem!

THE DIVINE RESCUE OPERATION

One of the greatest films of my lifetime has to be *Saving Private Ryan*. The year is 1944, June 6 at 0500 hours, and the outcome of the Second World War is in the balance. It is D-day, the day of the Allied forces landing on the beaches of Normandy. No film tells the story with more realism than that of *Saving Private Ryan*. It is not unusual to see elderly men weeping at the end of this movie—they are men who remember the horrors of war, some who were on Omaha Beach that day.

The sacrifice of these men is beyond description as they fought their way off the Higgins Boats to the beach to be caught in a virtual wall of withering, deadly fire from the cliffs above. The scene was one of chaos, mayhem, slaughter, confusion, and one of sacrifice, heroism, bravery, and the fight for survival and a foothold. First on the beach, then up the draws to the cliffs above, then through the countryside of France.

Captain John Miller, a schoolteacher from Pennsylvania was in the first wave to hit Omaha Beach. In the battle for the cliffs, Miller lost ninety-five men. It was a gruesome ordeal. Also on Omaha Beach that day was a Private Peter Ryan, who paid the ultimate sacrifice. On Utah Beach his brother Shawn Ryan paid the ultimate sacrifice. And in New Guinea, Daniel Ryan was killed. Three out of four brothers from a farm in Iowa, all killed in the span of a few days. Their fourth brother James Ryan was somewhere on the battlefields of France, among hundreds of thousands of other soldiers, having parachuted into Normandy.

The Department of Defense decided it had to find Private Ryan and get him out of combat before all four of his mother's boys were killed in the line of duty. Captain John Miller was tapped to take a squad of men and find Ryan and get him to safety. His job was nearly impossible. Find one man in the middle of an active war where the outcome of the action is in balance. Before Private Ryan is safe, many more men would die.

It is often only in retrospect that we fully appreciate the sacrifices made on our behalf. One of the most moving scenes in the film is when later in his life, in a Normandy graveyard, Ryan visits the grave of the man who saved him. In silence and with deep emotion, he knelt before the grave of the one who had saved him so many years before. I think he must have been silently asking, "Why me? Why did you pay the price to save me so I could live and experience a full life when you died in the process? How do I repay that kind of debt?"

The cross represents the most amazing rescue operation in all of history. Rather than walking away from His rebellious creation, God put into play a plan to redeem and reclaim what had been destroyed. And He did it by sending His own Son who would pay the price for mankind's rebellion by taking the penalty on Himself and dying in our place. The apostle Paul puts this in perspective for us.

> You see, at just the right time, when we were still power-less, Christ died for the ungodly. Very rarely will anyone die for a righteous man, though for a good man some-one might possibly dare to die. But God demonstrates his own love for us in this: While we were still sinners, Christ died for us. (Romans 5:6-8)

When Christ came to earth in the Incarnation, He invaded Satan's territory to rescue people lost in sin, one heart at a time, and as He did so, to take broken lives and bring wholeness through a personal relationship with Himself. Not only that, but it is His intention that His followers become instruments of God to bring hope, righteousness, love, grace, and help to others and to bring His justice and righteousness to the places we live and influence.

We looked at some of the descriptors of our world. Think about these descriptors of the kingdom Christ brought when He invaded history: love, joy, peace, patience, forgiveness, hope, holiness, purity, fairness, mercy, justice, goodness, grace, faith, humility, generosity, abundant life, freedom, new birth, power, restoration, healing, perseverance, kindness, service. When Jesus said He is the light of the world He gave us a wonderful picture of what happens when His kingdom invades a dark world through His people, who bring His character to a broken and hurting globe.

GOD'S D-DAY

D-day was the turning point in the war in Europe. From that day it was clear that the war would be won by the allies, but the war was not yet over. In the same way, the death and resurrection of Christ on the cross was the turning point in the divine drama between God and Satan. On the cross, Satan was decisively defeated, but until Christ returns in person to our planet, the struggle between the forces of evil and of heaven continues. Thus we continue to live in a fallen world but one that has been invaded by righteousness.

As Christ followers we therefore live with the tension that we have been redeemed by God and are now part of His family, but we still live in a world that suffers from the effects of the fall. We are destined for eternal life but are still subject to death. We know that the battle has been won but the war is not over.

Paul makes this clear when he tells us that "Our struggle is not against flesh and blood, but against the rulers, against the authorities, against the powers of this dark world and against the spiritual forces of evil in the heavenly realms" (Ephesians 6:12). We are redeemed and claimed and forgiven but we continue to live in a world ruled by the enemy. And a world that continues to suffer the scars of rebellion against God.

The cross is not the end of the story. In Revelation, John was given an amazing vision of what will one day be:

> Then I saw a new heaven and a new earth, for the first heaven and the first earth had passed away, and there was no longer any sea. I saw the Holy City, the new Jerusalem, coming down out of heaven from God, prepared as a bride beautifully dressed for her husband. And I heard a loud voice from the throne saying, "Now the dwelling of God is with men, and he will live with them. They will be his people, and God himself will be with them and be their God. He will wipe every tear from their eyes. There will be no more death or mourning or crying or pain, for the old order of things has passed away." He who was seated on the throne said, "I am making everything new! . . . Behold, I am coming soon!" (Revelation 21:1-5; 22:7).

Creation started as a perfect creation, and it will end as a perfect re-creation. Not only did God not abandon us, He will redeem what was ruined by sin. And notice that when He returns, life will never come undone, for there will be no more death or mourning or crying or pain. Not only that but the pain of the scars we live with today will be gone forever as He wipes every tear from our eyes. The old order will have passed away and God says, "I am making everything new!"

In that day, we will wear our scars with pride but there will be no pain, no sorrow, no mourning, and no pain. What was undone will be redone. What was deeply imperfect will then be amazingly perfect. What was lost will be reclaimed.

LIVING BETWEEN THE BOOKENDS OF CREATION AND RE-CREATION

Why do bad things happen to good people? We live between a perfect creation and a perfect re-creation, between two perfect bookends of history. But in the interim we live with the scars of a world undone—and our own lives are undone—until we invite Christ to become Lord of our life. And even then, we live in Satan's territory, temporarily, for Christ has overcome the world on the cross but until He returns in person, the scrimmages between the forces of good and evil continue. The divine D-day settled the matter, but the final battle has not been fought.

When I think of the cross, as Private Ryan at the grave of the one who gave his life for Him, I wonder, *why me?* Why would God care so much that He would give His life for me? Why would He reclaim men and women lost in sin? Why would He re-create what we destroyed? Why would He carry my brokenness on Himself in my place?

That is the real "why?" question when all is said and done. It is not, why do we suffer? It is, why does God redeem us and give us hope? It is not, why is life unfair? It is, why is God willing and wanting to enter into my situation with me?

Each of us who has made Jesus Lord of our lives is a trophy of His amazing grace. Listen to how Paul describes us:

> But because of his great love for us, God, who is rich in mercy, made us alive with Christ even when we were dead in transgressions—it is by grace you have been saved. And God raised us up with Christ and seated us with him in the heavenly realms in Christ Jesus, in order that in the coming ages he might show the incomparable

riches of his grace, expressed in his kindness to us in
Christ Jesus. (Ephesians 2:4-7)

In His divine rescue operation, God made us alive in Christ when
we were dead in our sinfulness. And then, while we continue to live
for a time in this broken world, we are figuratively already seated with
Jesus in heaven, for we are His children. Why? So that for all time, the
amazing love, mercy, and "incomparable riches of His grace" would be
evident for all to see.

As long as we live in this world we are the visible champions of
God's grace. As those who know us watch how we handle adversity,
pain, sorrow, and "life undone," they also see the hope that we have in
Jesus. That hope is clearly seen at the memorial services of those who
died with faith in Christ. There is sadness, but there is also celebration
for we know that our loved one is with Jesus. Compare that to those
services you have attended where that hope is not present. The difference
is amazing, and sad.

And here is where the truth that Jesus has "overcome the world"
becomes clear. We will have trouble in this world, but we can live with
His peace, and that peace is proof that He has indeed overcome the
world and won the war against evil. The divine D-day is only awaiting
the final inevitable outcome of Satan defeated and Jesus victorious. And
Eric will be there on that day, a new body, the dark night of the soul
replaced with unimaginable happiness and joy! A family reunited and
together for eternity!

BOLD PRAYER

Father, as Private Ryan bowing at the grave of the one who rescued
him, I bow before Your cross in amazement that You rescued me. I am
amazed that You would care and love and redeem me. I live in faith for
that day when the last vestige of evil in this world is defeated and a new
world remade by You is born. In the meantime, I thank You that I can
live with peace in the midst of trouble, for You have overcome the world.

QUESTIONS FOR DISCUSSION

Read John 10:1-18. How does Jesus describe Himself in relation to us and how does He describe the evil one?

John 10:10 is a key truth for this chapter. What are some of the ways that the evil one tries to steal, kill, and destroy? What are ways in which Jesus gives life and fullness of life to us?

Describe some ways that you have been impacted by "creation interrupted" but which God in His grace used to mold you into who you are today.

How do Paul's words in Ephesians 2:4-7 give us perspective in times of trouble?

CHAPTER FIVE

GOD'S AMAZING HEART
Understanding God's Love for Us

Does God care about our pain? By now we know the answer is yes: He profoundly cares. In fact it is ironic that we ask the question, because the truth is that there is no one who cares *more* about our situation than the Good Shepherd: Christ. He cared so much about the people He created that He created us in *His image*.

IMAGES OF GOD

I remember how proud and excited I was the day I brought my oldest son, Jon, home from the hospital. Everything had changed. I drove more carefully, I was protective of my baby and Mary Ann, a new sense of responsibility enveloped me.

As he began to grow and develop I started to recognize some of me in him and it warmed my heart. Jon is a combination of Mary Ann and me; in many ways he is our image, even though he is a unique individual in his own right. Any mother knows the awesome miracle of a child that has come from her womb. The bond between mother and child is a deep and profound one.

There is a mystery in creation that will remain a mystery until we see God face-to-face. When He chose to create men and women, why did He choose to create them after His own image? Here is God, the one who has no beginning and no end, who is three persons in one, living in perfect unity and fellowship (God the Father, God the Son, and God the Holy Spirit), who is divine, holy (morally pure), transcendent (above all things), sovereign (has all power), and yet He chooses to make men and women in His image! None of the rest of creation was made in His image—just men and women!

In making us in His image, God gave to us a dignity, an importance, a kinship with Him that is unique and unparalleled. Just as Jon has "me" in Him, God planted something of "Him" in us that made us unique, important, precious to Him. We are not random creatures here by fate to be buffeted by the capricious winds of history. We are men and women, precious to God, known by God, and made in His very image.

What does it mean that we were made in His image? First, it means that we could have intimate relationship and fellowship with the eternal God of the universe, and what's more astonishing, He desired (and still does) that relationship. Just as the Father, the Son, and the Holy Spirit have fellowship with each other, we can have fellowship with one another and with Him.

Second, we were created with a moral dimension unlike the rest of creation. We were created with the ability to choose holy and moral actions over immoral and evil actions. That is why, even after the Fall, we sense guilt and shame when we do something we know to be wrong. We have a built-in moral compass.

Third, we have a desire to connect with God. You see that desire wherever you travel in the world, whether it is in Buddhists trying to achieve a higher level of consciousness; Hindus seeking to please or appease one of the forty million plus gods of Hinduism; Muslims seeking to achieve paradise; animists trying to appease the spirits in the rocks, hills, and trees; or even New Age varieties where some kind of connection with the divine and eternal is the goal. That desire to connect is nothing other than the residue of a perfect creation, now marred by sin, but the dim perfection of the original creation still echoes down through humanity in a yearning for relationship with the transcendent.

All of this can be summed up by a certain majesty and glory that God created when He created men and women. Which is why the Fall and the destruction brought by sin is so sad. The thief came to destroy all that God created and we are infected and affected by sin and the Fall.

What we cannot lose sight of is the amazing dignity that God created in men and women in His original creation. He has an undying love for His creation that motivated Him never to abandon even sinful creatures, but to launch the divine rescue operation we explored in the last chapter.

There is *nothing* God will not do to win His creatures back—those made in His image—including the death of His own Son on the cross to pay our penalty and restore our relationship. That is what we mean to Him. That is why there is no sin He will not willingly forgive, no guilt He will not willingly remove, no life He will not gladly redeem. He *wants* us back. We were meant for Him and He loves you and me with an undying, amazing, and eternal love.

If you are a parent, you know something about that kind of love. What would you not do for your son or daughter, made in your image? Even when they go their own way, do their own thing, inflict pain on parents, we want them back, we love them dearly—they are ours. We are God's and He loves us with that same parental, undying love, even when we stray and cause His heart pain. Why does God love us? Why will God intervene on our behalf? Why does He welcome even prodigals back and welcome them warmly? He made us for fellowship with Himself. He made us in His image. He loves us with an undying love. We were made for Him!

IN THE IMAGE OF MAN

How much does God love us?

In making man in His image, God gave great honor to those He created. In fact, there is no greater honor that could be bestowed by our Creator. But that image was deeply marred by sin, and the fellowship God so deeply desired with His creations was destroyed. Under the influence of Satan, man had rejected the gift God had so graciously bestowed. No longer were we in fellowship with God but rather sentenced to death for our rebellion.

In response, God did the unthinkable and unimaginable. The One who had made us in His image, sent His Son to our sinful world now made in *our* image. The Creator was now a creature. The One who lived as a spirit, now took on a human body. The One who had ruled and roamed the universe was now confined to a body, gravity, illness, suffering, hunger, sorrow, fatigue, friendships, betrayal, family, and all the circumstances of humanity—and finally death.

One is amazed that God would make us in His image, but one cannot comprehend that God would send His son in *our* image. Never had a greater reversal of roles taken place! Yet "The Word became flesh and made his dwelling among us. We have seen his glory, the glory of the One and Only, who came from the Father, full of grace and truth" (John 1:14). Now the unapproachable God could be approached and seen and known and understood. As John wrote, "No one has ever seen God, but God the One and Only, who is at the Father's side, has made him known [through Jesus]" (John 1:18).

One of the most frustrating experiences for someone walking through pain is encounters with those who have never experienced life undone—yet. Well meaning words are spoken (It will be okay. God is good. I understand. Just have faith.), words that hurt and frustrate because we know they come from someone who has never experienced the deep pain we are in. The truth is that a hug and comforting presence is far more meaningful than many words.

But this is where the great reversal—when the Creator took on our image—changes our perspective of God. Jesus experienced the kinds of things we experience. The writer of Hebrews said,

> During the days of Jesus' life on earth, he offered up prayers and petitions with loud cries and tears to the one who could save him from death, and he was heard because of his reverent submission. Although he was a son, he learned obedience from what he suffered and, once made perfect, he became the source of eternal salvation for all who obey him. (Hebrews 5:7-10)

And again,

> Therefore, since we have a great high priest who has gone through the heavens, Jesus the Son of God, let us hold firmly to the faith we profess. For we do not have a high priest who is unable to sympathize with our weaknesses, but we have one who has been tempted in every way, just as we are—yet was without sin. Let us then approach the throne of grace with confidence, so that we may receive mercy and find grace to help us in our time of need. (Hebrews 4:14-16)

It is precisely because Jesus has walked in our shoes that He can understand our situations, and because He is God He can give us the mercy and grace we need in our time of need. All because He loved us enough to make us in His image and when His image in us was marred by sin, to take on our image so that we could know Him, relate to Him, and through His death for our sin, once again be in fellowship with Him. How much does God love us? Enough to do the unthinkable in order to save us, know us, and be with us.

THE DIVINE TOUCH

There is nothing that Jesus loves to do more than touch those who are hurting! There is a wonderful account in Luke 5 that demonstrates the heart of Jesus toward us:

> While Jesus was in one of the towns, a man came along who was covered with leprosy. When he saw Jesus, he fell with his face to the ground and begged him, "Lord, if you are willing, you can make me clean." (Luke 5:12)

In ancient Israel, leprosy was considered the worst disease one could have. No leper was allowed to live inside the city; they were relegated to a place for lepers outside the city gates. No one was allowed to touch a leper, and when they walked on the road they were required to call out "I am a leper" to warn those on the road to stay away. They were considered unclean, sinners, dirty, and were the scum of society. They ranked lower than tax collectors and prostitutes.

One thing this man knew was that Jesus could cure him from leprosy. He had probably seen Jesus cure others and His reputation was well known. The crowd around Jesus was probably scandalized that this unclean man had the audacity to call out to Jesus, "Lord, if you are willing, you can make me clean."

Even more astonishing to the crowd was what Jesus did next. "Jesus reached out his hand and touched the man. 'I am willing,' he said. 'Be clean!' And immediately the leprosy left him" (Luke 5:13). What would have astonished the crowd is not that Jesus healed the leper—they had seen Him heal many people of their sickness. Nor that He was willing, for Jesus never turned any away looking for help. What amazed them was that Jesus actually physically *touched* the leper.

Here was a man who had not felt a human touch for as long as he was a leper. Imagine not having any human contact with another. No hugs, no kiss, no handshakes, no tender touch on the shoulder, no embrace. Jesus could have simply given the word that he was healed, but Jesus chose to give this man not only the gift of healing but His divine physical touch. For as long as he lived, that man would never forget the *touch*. I believe it meant as much to him as the fact he had been healed. It is what he needed and it is what Jesus gave.

Jesus loves to *touch* our lives in ways we need and when we need it. He does so in ways that remind us of His love and presence. Often it is through other people who are His hands, feet, words, and love to us. Sometimes it is through circumstances that only He could orchestrate. Sometimes it is a word He speaks to us or a peace He gives to us.

One evening in December 2007, while I was in a coma and my situation was grave, my youngest sister, Deb, who often sat with me during the night, was standing next to the ventilator feeling angry with God for allowing this illness to threaten my life. She was tired, discouraged, and questioning God with the "why" questions. Suddenly she sensed that she was not alone, felt an arm on her shoulder and instantly knew that it would be okay, *whatever* happened to me. It was an instantaneous okay, whether I lived or died. She instinctively looked around to see who the touch came from and no one was there. But she knew that she had been touched by God or an angelic being.

God touched my friend Grant. He lost his twin brother on June 20, many years ago, when he was killed along with his fiancée in a helicopter accident. Not only did he lose his closest friend but his brother did not know Christ. That fact has been a driving factor in Grant's life since he became a Christ follower—to do all he can to ensure that others find Christ and have the opportunity his twin did not.

Years later, Grant, as the CFO of a major corporation was central in negotiating the company's sale. It was a long and torturous process that hung at times by a thread. The day it sold was June 20. Grant realized that this was no coincidence but that God had not only given to him means beyond his imagination but resources that he was to steward for the purpose of evangelism. He felt the *touch* of God that day, and he immediately knew the purpose of God for the assignment God had given him.

Mary Ann and I have been touched by God through other people more times than I can enumerate. We have prayed for needs together and seen those needs answered. We have experienced the love, help, and provision of others, some of whom had no knowledge of our needs but felt prompted by God to do something. This has led us to be intentional in showing that love of God to others whenever and wherever we can. Jesus loves to touch lives, and we want to join Him in touching the lives of others. As recipients of His lavish grace, we want to be purveyors of that grace. His touch through us!

Where do you need the touch of God today? He wants to give it to you! All you need to do is ask and believe that He will enter into your situation, your crisis, your undone*ness* with His touch in His creative way. He wants to surprise you just like he surprised the leper—by giving you what you need at this moment of your life. Take a moment and think back to times when you have felt the clear touch of God on your life that brought you encouragement and hope.

As the writer of Hebrews wrote, "Let us then approach the throne of grace with confidence, so that we may receive mercy and find grace to help us in our time of need" (Hebrews 4:16). He is waiting, ready, and longs to meet us with His grace in our area of need.

If one wants to understand God's heart for us, all one has to do is to look at the blessing that God gave the priests in the Old Testament. These are the words they were to bless the Israelites with, and it is God's heart for you. This is a blessing that one can "soak" in on a bad day! It is one that everyone should memorize and meditate on.

> The LORD bless you and keep you;
> The LORD make his face shine upon you and be
> gracious to you;
> The LORD turn his face toward you and give you peace.
> (Numbers 6:24-26)

God intends to bless you—today! Even though you cannot see it, God's face is shining on you and He is being gracious to you. And because His face is turned toward you and the situation you face, He can give you peace—the same promise we have seen Jesus make—peace in the midst of the trouble we face in this world.

Knowing that God's face and heart is turned in my direction—and yours—when life comes undone makes all the difference. I was not alone in the Thailand ICU! God's face was turned toward me, His face was shining on my situation, and in His graciousness He gave me His peace.

When we left the hospital we went back to the ICU to give a gift to each of the nurses and aids who had ministered to me. Through a translator they said, "we've never had a patient or a family like this. It was very different from what we normally have. We don't understand it!" What they had experienced was the peace, graciousness, and the face of God turned toward us in the middle of a terrible situation. They did not understand, but they experienced something very different. The difference was the wonderful, loving, attentive heart of God shining on us. It overflowed to them even as it ministered to me.

GOD'S OVERFLOW

One of the gifts of suffering is that those who have suffered much are most able to minister to others who suffer. There is an understanding, a kinship of those who have suffered, and those who have experienced the dark night of the soul have a unique ability to minister.

Years ago, the first time that life came undone for me, I experienced deep clinical depression that took a long toll on my life. As I healed from that experience, I noticed that I could spot others who were living with depression; often, they didn't realize the darkness that was encompassing them. My experience gave me the opportunity to help others who were walking through depression.

Paul tells us that one of the purposes of suffering is that it allows us to minister to others who suffer:

> Praise be to the God and Father of our Lord Jesus Christ, the Father of compassion and the God of all comfort, who comforts us in all our troubles, so that we can comfort those in any trouble with the comfort we ourselves have received from God. For just as the sufferings of Christ flow over into our lives, so also through Christ our comfort overflows. If we are distressed, it is for your comfort and salvation; if we are comforted, it is for your comfort, which produces in you patient endurance of the same sufferings we suffer. And our hope for you is firm, because we know that just as you share in our sufferings, so also you share in our comfort. (2 Corinthians 1:3-7)

I love the names that Paul uses for God: "*The Father of compassion and the God of all comfort.*" There is no one more compassionate than God. Compassion is the ability to understand and enter into our situation in a way that God actually feels what we feel and suffers when we suffer. Because He is the "God of all comfort" and has literally entered into our pain, He is able to bring comfort to our situation.

It was that comfort I experienced when on the ventilator and in great pain in Thailand. It was that comfort that Mary Ann experienced as she flew halfway around the world, wondering if I would be alive when she arrived. God's comfort is not cheap words but a comfort that comes out of His own suffering and entering into our suffering as the Father of compassion.

It is *this* comfort that those who don't know Jesus cannot understand when they see it in Christ followers. Think of the difference between the attitudes of those who know Jesus and those who are trying to deal with suffering on their own. Both are suffering, but the one who knows Christ has a divine Friend alongside them, and it makes all the difference.

Why does God comfort us in our troubles? So that we can comfort those in any trouble with the comfort we ourselves have received from God. For just as the sufferings of Christ flow over into our lives, so also through Christ our comfort overflows (see 2 Corinthians 1:4-5). The very comfort that overflows from God into our lives overflows from us into the lives of others who also suffer.

The Christ followers who have suffered much are usually the ones who can encourage other fellow sufferers the most. One rarely hears them complain. There is a depth to their faith that comes from deep reliance on God. They have a joy that makes no sense but it comes out of their closeness to God. The encouragement and perspective God gives them overflows to others. It is one of the great gifts that those who have suffered can give to others. It comes out of a deep well of understanding, empathy, compassion, trust, and reliance on a faithful God. They have walked the hard trail and have become the guides to others who are walking the hard trail.

My dear friend Doug walked the path of ALS for the last five years of his life. What amazed me was the steadfast faith he had in God in spite of the way the disease robbed him of so many things he enjoyed doing. He was realistic and honest but you always left his presence feeling encouraged by *him*. God's comfort to him overflowed in comfort to others. People wanted to be with him because they were ministered to in his presence. God's overflow!

I want to be one of those "overflow" people who hurting people gravitate to because they sense in me a kindred spirit—one who understands, one who encourages, and one who provides the comfort of Christ because of the comfort He has provided me. Just as those who have been forgiven much understand God's grace better than others, so those who have suffered much understand God's comfort better than others. They also understand what the dark night of the soul feels like and can, like Jesus, empathize because they have been there.

In the last eighteen months, after my two long bouts in the ICU, numerous people have come to me to ask me to pray for them about their situation. Why? Because they know I understand what life undone is like. They saw God meet me in my need in miraculous ways and they want that touch from God as well. I am a walking billboard of God's grace and mercy—and so are you! Without a second thought, today I will put my hand on someone's shoulder and pray for them or encourage them. From the overflow of God's comfort and goodness to me, I am able to pass it on to others. So can you. It is an amazing gift to those who are in the midst of pain. We become the carriers of the amazing heart of God!

BOLD PRAYER

Father, I thank You for Your amazing heart of love toward me. I thank You for becoming one with me through the Incarnation so that I can approach You with the confidence that You understand me and my circumstances. You are not a distant God but one who comforts me in my troubles. I pray that when Your sufferings flow over into my life, Your comfort would come as well, and that I could in turn comfort others with Your comfort. Finally, I pray the great prayer from the Old Testament that You would bless me and keep me. That You would make Your face to shine upon me and be gracious to me. That You would turn Your face toward me and give me peace. Amen.

QUESTIONS FOR DISCUSSION

Have you ever experienced a "divine touch" from God? What did that feel like and how did it encourage you?

Read Hebrews 4:14-16 and 5:7-10. How should the "divine reversal," where the Creator became a creature, impact our view of His ability to help us deal with "life undone"?

How can God use our pain to minister to others in pain according to 2 Corinthians 1:3-7? Can you think of times when this was true in your experience?

How have you personally experienced God's amazing heart toward you?

CHAPTER SIX

HIGH ROPES AND WATERFALLS
Where Faith and Grace Collide
Mary Ann Addington

When our son Steven was in fifth grade I was asked to be a parent volunteer on a three-day class trip to Wolfridge Environmental Learning Center in northeast Minnesota. One of our activities was a high-ropes course. Starting from a walk across a balance beam type of structure, the course builds up to a thirty-foot-high Burma Bridge, and ends in a zip line ride back to the ground.

The Burma Bridge was the most intimidating because one walks across on a single cable. Even being hooked into a cable above your head and cables at your side, you still have to step out onto the single line. After I coaxed and encouraged about ten fifth graders to go over the Burma Bridge, one youngster turned to me and said, "Mrs. Addington! Now it is your turn!"

This was not what I had signed up for, but I could hardly chicken out after telling all the kids that they could do it. As I was on the platform trying to figure out if there was any way out of stepping onto the cable, my fan club stood below. "Mrs. Addington, we know you can do it!" "Come on, Mrs. Addington, you helped us do it!" With trepidation I took my first step out, the cable held, and the line above was still hooked in. About halfway across I even breathed enough to notice that above the trees I could see Lake Superior off in the distance. And to the delight of my fan club below, I actually made it across the cable and back to terra firma.

THE HIGH-WIRE OF FAITH

Living by faith when life comes undone is much like walking the Burma Bridge. The wobbling cable is hard to walk, it is a long way down, and every step forward requires balance and the faith that the cable will hold and the safety ropes can be trusted. The first steps are the hardest, but there comes a place where we actually start to breathe again. While we would never willingly sign up for it, we learn that we can take the step of faith, put our weight on the line, and that the cable will hold the safety ropes.

Living on the wire of faith means sticking to the confidence that God is in control and can be trusted even when *all* evidence is to the contrary. During T.J.'s initial illness, I would be irritated with people who would say over and over how hard this must have been on his dad because he was a doctor and understood how sick Tim was.

I would think, "This is true, but give me some credit!" I am an RN with ER and ICU experience, and I had done of lot of research on MRSA and ARDS. I knew that this was really, really bad. There were numbers on his monitor that were worse than I had ever seen—except on someone who was dying. I could tell by the body language of the nursing and medical staff that they thought I was in la-la land when I spoke of discharge planning.

Every night I would go to sleep listening to Lincoln Brewster's "Another Hallelujah," and I had to tell God that this would be my response to whatever happened the next day. Every day was like taking another step of faith on the high ropes, choosing to trust God. I had to train myself to move from fear to trust countless times during the long ICU ordeal. "Fear not" is the most repeated command in all of Scripture because it is so easy to live in fear rather than in faith. It is a choice we make, and it is really about whether we focus on our undone*ness* or on our God.

My worst day in T.J.'s first ordeal in the ICU was when I received a call from his sister telling me to get to his room right away because his stats were crashing. I rushed back to the hospital from a nearby restaurant to find T.J.'s heart beating at 240 beats per minute. This was on top of his massive pneumonia, ARDS, septic shock, and a failed mitral valve in his heart. His heart was desperately trying to compensate for the mitral valve failure and get oxygen to his organs.

The nurses hustled me out of the room so they could try to shock his heart back into rhythm. I went to a nearby room where I could see what was happening, overwhelmed with fear. This was the worst it could be. Humanly speaking, T.J.'s heart would just give up. They could not do surgery to mend the mitral valve because he would not survive the surgery. It was God's intervention, or death. And that intervention had to be quick. There were *no* other options.

Sitting in that alcove watching the medical personnel around T.J.'s bed, I desperately wrestled with fear and faith in a way I had never done before. God had told me that it would be close, but he would make it (more about that later). Could I really believe that in the face of what I was watching? Was that rational? Could God really be trusted? Had I heard Him right? This was one of those instances when the medical personnel would not even make eye contact with me because they knew the inevitable outcome. Indescribable fear gripped my whole body. I felt like I was about to go into a free fall from the high-wire and there were no safety lines attached.

I *chose* faith over fear, as hard as that was watching what I was watching. The staff was not able to shock T.J.'s heart back into rhythm, and we knew that unless the mitral valve was healed there was no way he would survive. We put out an urgent call for a day of prayer and fasting specifically asking for a miracle to heal the mitral valve. Across the globe those watching the blog (over 10,000 individual users) stormed the gates of heaven boldly asking for an outright miracle. Within that twenty-four-hour period it started to heal! He was not out of the woods by any means, but God was true to the words He had given me.

To this day, when T.J. visits his cardiologist, he shakes his head and says, "How did you dodge that bullet?" They were certain that he would need surgery to repair the valve when he was well enough to have it—if he survived. On his most recent visit, the cardiologist told T.J. he did not need to come back.

One of the hard things is that God does not always do what we wish He would do. His ways are sovereign, and we will not always understand His plans or purposes for our lives. But we always have the choice of focusing on Him or focusing on our circumstances. Our circumstances are unpredictable, but He is always faithful. It is the choice we make between fear and faith when life comes undone.

God loves it when we *choose* to trust Him! And it is as much a choice as when we put our full weight on the cable and begin that hard walk. Trusting does not mean that we know how everything will turn out, but that we live in the confidence that God loves us like we love our kids and that He is in control.

Trusting God brings peace, even when that does not seem logical. Isaiah 26:3 has been posted on my bathroom mirror since December of 2007:

> You will keep in perfect peace
> him whose mind is steadfast,
> because he trusts in you.

It is not about me! It is about keeping my mind and emotions focused on who God is. It is not about whether I have done all the right things, or even that I am trusting the right way. It is about keeping our minds steadfast on who God said He is and what He has promised to do, which includes giving us peace when all evidence says that cannot happen. Life on the high ropes is not about us—it is all about God, His grace, and our simple trust in Him. It's putting our weight on the wire one step at a time.

GOD SPEAKS OUR LANGUAGE

Our oldest son, Jon, lived in China the year after high school, studying Chinese and doing tech support for an NGO. One day he went into a store and asked the clerk in Chinese to help him find something. The clerk looked at another employee and said, "I don't know English, do you know what he wants?" The other clerk said something to the effect,

"He is speaking *Chinese*, stupid!" Because he did not expect to hear Chinese from this young Anglo, he didn't recognize his own language!

Sometimes I think we don't hear God because we don't think He speaks our language. We don't really *expect* Him to answer directly when we pray. Prior to seeing God work so powerfully in healing T.J., my own prayer was more like wishing rather than expecting. I would talk at God, *wishing* that He would do something. I frankly lacked the confidence that I really was *good enough* to ask God for big things.

Have you ever felt unworthy to ask God to answer your real needs? This is where grace and faith collide! The great giant of the faith, Daniel, understood this truth. In one of the great prayers of the Old Testament, Daniel said, "We do not make requests of you because we are righteous, but because of your great mercy" (Daniel 9:18). Living on the high-wire of faith is actually believing that God hears us because He said He would hear us and answer based on His *mercy*, not on any *worthiness* (or unworthiness) on our part. God wants me to ask for big things because He is honored when He can show His power. And He loves His kids!

Several days into T.J.'s first hospitalization I was sitting in his room in the ICU thinking that this was going to be ugly. As I watched T.J. struggling to breath, I specifically asked God to show me how to pray. Immediately I heard back as clearly as if a human voice had spoken to me, "It is going to be really close, but he is going to make it." Our son Jon came into the room almost immediately and said, "Did you just feel a real peace come over this room?" I told him what I had just heard.

Other people who were close to us, including our prayer team, confirmed it, and we were in a situation where I could not afford to second-guess God. (Did you really say that? Do you really talk to us? Can I trust that this is from you?) God also sent a lot of encouragement to stay on the high-wire of trust, and I believed that He was going to act.

One evening T.J.'s nurse was checking all of his equipment (nine IVs, a feeding tube, a monitor with several wires, a chest tube, cooling blanket, and of course, the ventilator), and she left the room rather abruptly. She told me later that as she was assessing all the stuff, she was overcome with the absolute knowledge that T.J. was going to survive. She started to cry and said, "God just told me that he is going to be okay!" Many of the people who followed the blog told us that God repeatedly gave them the confidence that He was doing a miracle.

I realized in a new way that God not only speaks my language but that He could speak very specifically to me about the situation I faced, and it was His voice that I could hold onto.

WATERFALLS OF GRACE

Big Sky, Montana, is our favorite place to vacation. We read, hike, fly-fish, and relax in the shadow of the Spanish Peaks and Lone Mountain. In the summer of 2007 I realized that I did not really understand God's grace and embarked on a word study of grace during my personal quiet time. Little did I know that this was part of God's preparation for what was ahead of us.

I had printed off sheets from Bible Gateway [http://www.biblegate-way.com/] and took a couple of the sheets on a walk up the Ousel Falls trail. When I came to the end of the paved trail, I took a narrow path that leads to the top of the falls, and I climbed out to sit on a rock a few feet into the stream to ponder grace.

The falls is one of the forks of the Gallatin River (*A River Runs Through It*, although I have never seen Brad Pitt on the river) and sitting above the falls the power of the water is deceptive before it crashes down to a pristine pool in the narrow canyon below. I could see a rock on the other side of the river that formed a shallow oblong bowl just below the surface of the water. It was a hot day, and it seemed that if it were possible to actually get across the river, that rock would be a perfect place to lie down and let the water rush over and around you. It would be awesome to be refreshed and cleansed and feel the power of the water. This is a picture of grace. God's grace combines power, refreshment, and cleansing. There is nothing we can do to change it, control it, or stop it.

I like rules, probably because I was always good at them (those who know T.J. know that he is very bad at them). I was an unabashed brown-noser in school and got good grades and nice comments from teachers on my report cards, so rules worked for me. I have my own unofficial rules for how you ought to drive (Hey, blonde chick, stay off my tail!); how to shop (get your cart out of the middle of the aisle); and how to pray (ACTS: adoration, confession, thanksgiving, and supplication). I am not knocking the acronym, but somehow I had boiled prayer down to rules and not about talking to the God of the universe about what is on my heart. Understanding grace helped me believe that I could pray boldly because the hinge pin is God's grace and mercy—not if I am doing it right or worthy to be heard.

In February of 2008, T.J. was well enough to be safe at home alone, and I went back to work at the large public high school where I was the nurse. Within a week I had a constant migraine, was short of breath, and exhausted. It turns out there was a sprinkler head leak in the building when T.J. was in the hospital, and it resulted in mold in the building. I have a severe mold allergy.

After the building was remediated over spring break, I went back to work, and again, within a week, could not stay in the building. It became apparent that I could not continue in this job—in fact, my doctor would not allow me to go back into the building even to collect my stuff. I also seemed to get sick from every virus that blew by my nose. In June I told God that I thought we deserved to be "graduated." Surely we had learned what He was teaching us and had earned a break. I was ready to get off the Burma Bridge.

The next several months were a combination of frustration and grace. In August we were back in Big Sky to reclaim our fitness. Instead, a ruptured disc in T.J.'s neck became excruciatingly painful and we spent a lot of our time and energy trying to make him comfortable. When we got back home, there had been a leak in the front of our house, and there was mold in our laundry room. We stayed with friends while the house was cleaned up. T.J.'s brother headed a volunteer crew to re-side the front of our house and paint the rest of it. Our dishwasher broke, the floor drain in the laundry room backed up (I freak with water in the house because of mold), the dryer quit working, mysterious wet spots would appear on the floor in the laundry room, the garage door opener rebelled, and I can't remember everything else—except for the time when the doorknob in the bathroom broke, and T.J. was stuck inside the bathroom. He had to unscrew his way out with a finger nail clipper.

T.J. also had neck surgery and then fell and broke his tailbone. This was getting ridiculous, but with every frustrating event, God met our needs. In December things looked like they were quieting down when T.J. and Chip went to Thailand where T.J. again ended up on a ventilator. In March I developed blood clots in my lungs and was rushed to the ER. While working up the clots I was diagnosed with an unrelated liver issue, and my social life in April and May revolved around doctors and medical tests.

Sometimes we have to stay on the rope and depend on grace a lot longer than we want to. Sometimes life just sucks, but God is still good!

As I look back over the past twenty months, I am amazed at the grace that has washed over our lives through God's faithfulness and other people's love. Every word of encouragement is His grace. Each time my fear was replaced by His peace was grace. Countless acts of love by others were His grace. Like the Ousel Falls, God's grace has swirled around our lives in amazing ways.

One of the unexpected gifts of hard times is that we experience His grace in ways we have never experienced before! As T.J. often says, "It is a wonderful thing to come to the place where all we have is God." The process of getting there is painful, but the realization of God's goodness, mercy, love, and grace is worth the pain. I will never be the same for walking through the past twenty months. I have changed, my heart for God is deeper, my walk of faith is surer, my prayer life is bolder, and my understanding of God's power has moved from the intellectual to the personal.

The difficult times in life are about what God is molding me to. Life on the high ropes is not remedial but rather it is formative. God is making my heart like His. I can't tell you if we are at the end of this particular high ropes, but I can tell you that I would never trade the appreciation I have for God's grace and the richness of knowing that He intervenes in my life for living on the ground.

WHEN GRACE AND FAITH COLLIDE

There is no more powerful combination than grace and faith. In fact, our level of faith is dependent on our understanding of grace. One of the lessons I learned through T.J.'s illnesses is that I *had* to live by faith because I had no other options. But faith required me to grapple with grace, which is why God had me on the track of grace just before life came undone for us.

Faith requires us to believe that God is in our corner and has unconditional love for us. As long as I thought God's response to me was based on my own *worthiness,* I was in trouble, because I could never be worthy enough. And if I was not worthy, then how could I pray boldly or even believe that He would hear and answer?

I believe many of us fall into the trap of believing that we need to earn God's favor, when, in fact, there is nothing we can do to cause God to love us more than He does, and there is nothing we can do to cause Him to love us less than He does. Once I surrender my life to Him in faith, I live in His grace. Grace is by definition, undeserved favor. God is by definition an infinite God with infinite favor, so as His child I am the recipient of an infinite amount of undeserved favor and grace that cascades over my life like Ousel Falls.

Living in His favor means that I no longer need to try to earn His favor. In fact, it cannot be earned, which is why it is called *grace.* But it also means that I can talk to Him about anything, knowing that He loves me, hears me, and responds to my prayer. And, most amazing of all, that He wants to talk to *me* and show me His amazing love.

When life comes undone there are no more important gifts than faith and grace. In grace I can rest assured that God has my best interests in mind—always. In faith I can bring my brokenness to Him for His intervention. Because of grace I know that I don't need to prove my worthiness to Him. Because of faith I know that He can be trusted in those high-wire moments.

Whatever your situation today I want to encourage you to bask in the grace of God. He loves you unconditionally. He honors *every* move you make toward Him, no matter how small or tentative. He suffers when you suffer and laughs when you laugh. His face is turned toward you in love (see Numbers 6:26). He wants to be your help, encouragement, and peace today. He desires that you crawl up in His lap as your Daddy (see Romans 8:15; Galatians 4:6). Nothing can separate you from His love and presence (see Romans 8:38-39). His grace is always greater than your sin (see Romans 5:20-21). His love is infinite and His regard for you unrivaled. He has given you gifts that you cannot even imagine (see Ephesians 3:20), and in a figurative sense, you already sit with Jesus in heaven (see Ephesians 2:6). You are a trophy of His grace (see Ephesians 2:6-7). Do you get it? You are in the waterfall of His grace if you have made Him the Lord of your life.

Because of that amazing grace, you can come to Him in faith to get you across whatever Burma Bridge you face. On the high-wire, He is there. You can approach Him with bold requests (see Hebrews 4:16). You can trust Him completely. You can ask boldly and know that He has the power to intervene in miraculous ways. Even when His answer is not the answer you were looking for, you can have the confidence that He is in control and nothing in His control can ever be out of control.

Most of all, I want to encourage you to take the time to be with Him and to allow Him to minister to you and encourage your heart. Be attentive to the grace He has already showered upon you. No matter how bad your personal situation, God is infinitely good and His goodness always outweighs the weight of our undone*ness*.

On the high-wire, as long as I looked down, I felt fear. When I looked up and saw the trees and Lake Superior in the distance, I saw beauty. When we take the time to be with God and take our eyes off our own situation, we see His grace and the beauty of what He is doing in and through us. It is a matter of perspective. Are we looking down in fear or up in faith?

Grace and faith are what is most needed when life comes undone. When grace and faith collide, the result is amazing and powerful! Allow them to collide in your life today.

BOLD PRAYER

Father I thank You that Your grace and my faith can collide in a powerful way when walking through suffering and uncertainty. I claim all of the grace I need for this day and ask for the faith that I need today. I ask this not on the basis of my goodness but on the basis of Your favor—just like Daniel. Thank You that I don't need to earn Your favor but can just relax in the waterfall of Your grace. In the process of my "high-wire" experiences would You mold my heart to become more like Yours! Amen.

QUESTIONS FOR DISCUSSION

Describe situations in your life where your faith and God's grace have collided in a powerful way. How did His grace in your situation change your perspective or encourage you?

Read 1 Peter 1:3-9. How does God use difficult times to mold our hearts and change us? Can you give an example from your own life where your heart became more like His through tough times?

Have you ever been reticent to pray boldly, as Mary Ann writes, because you feel that you are unworthy of God responding to your request? How does Daniel 9:18 and Hebrews 4:16 change that equation for you?

Consider making a list of God's grace in your life that came directly out of difficult times.

CHAPTER SEVEN

STORMING HEAVEN'S GATES
Bold Prayer

Life undone requires bold faith! And *big* requests! When on the high-wire, there are no other good options. For us there were *no* other options—period. The following are taken from the blog: reachtj.blogspot.com.

December 4, 2007: T.J. enters the ICU unable to breath.

December 6: Significant pneumonia in the left lung is confirmed along with a pleural effusion. Massive antibiotics are failing to stop the spread of pneumonia.

December 7: 650 ccs are drained from the pleural effusion on T.J.'s left side.

December 8: T.J. is put on a ventilator into an induced coma after he is unable to handle the stress of breathing. There is a close brush with death when the breathing tube kinks when being inserted and T.J. cannot breath. Antibiotics continue to fail to stem the tide of pneumonia.

December 10: It is confirmed that T.J. has MRSA, his fever rises past 102, and a TEE (Trans Esophageal Echocardiogram) shows that a mitral valve is leaking badly. The family publicly asks people to pray for miraculous healing of the valve. Another 550 ccs are drained from a pleural effusion.

December 12: A chest X-ray shows the pneumonia starting to spread to the upper right lobe, sedation is increased, temperature starts to fluctuate, and blood pressure remains low.

December 13: The doctors' worst fears start to develop. T.J. is put on 100 percent oxygen with vent pressure turned to its highest setting.

His breathing becomes more difficult, he goes into septic shock, and his blood pressure continues to be troublesome.

December 16: T.J. starts to have pre-atrial contractions and his heart rate hits an impressive 235 bpm. Shocking him doesn't work, medication is given and the heart rate comes back down, but the doctor says he honestly doesn't know whether the drop was from prayer or the medication.

December 17: A new TEE shows the mitral valve leak to be moderate rather than severe now, the O2 was lowered to 60 percent during the night, giving T.J. some margin. Both lungs are significantly inflamed. T.J. has ARDS, and the doctors are looking hard for the secondary infection.

December 18: A new TEE shows the mitral valve to be practically just fine.

December 22: While T.J. is still weaning well, his slowness in waking up becomes a concern. Moreover, it is discovered that he has a massive blood clot covering three veins, including his jugular, subclavian, and one in his right arm. These are all places where the PIC line (aka catheter, swan line) were put in.

December 23: T.J.'s vitals are OK; he is looking responsive but nothing that would qualify clinically as responsive.

December 25: Still slowly getting better and appearing more alert, but not following any commands.

December 27: T.J. won't follow commands for the doctors, but will occasionally for Mary Ann. He appears to understand the news on CNN.

It would be eighteen more days in the hospital before I would be home. From the time I went into the hospital, God raised people up around the globe to storm heaven's gates on my behalf and plead for my life and recovery. That in itself was an amazing work that only God could have done. One of the common stories on the blog was that God was waking people up at 3:00 a.m. in different time zones around the world to pray.

A consistent theme of the blog responses was how the faith of those who were watching and praying was strengthened as time after time God chose to intervene miraculously to preserve my life. Some 10,000 unique users were watching the blog from 78 countries and 50 states. It was as if God Himself raised up an army of faithful prayer warriors to pray and to show all of us His amazing power to heal against all odds. It was nothing less than a worldwide movement of bold faith.

BOLD FAITH

In Luke 11, Jesus taught his disciples how to pray with The Lord's Prayer. It is a bold prayer with bold requests. But then Jesus goes on to expand His teaching on prayer:

> Then he said to them, "Suppose one of you has a friend, and he goes to him at midnight and says, "Friend, lend me three loaves of bread, because a friend of mine on a journey has come to me, and I have nothing to set before him."
>
> Then the one inside answers, "Don't bother me. The door is already locked, and my children are with me in bed. I can't get up and give you anything." I tell you, though he will not get up and give him the bread because he is his friend, yet *because of the man's boldness* he will get up and give him as much as he needs.
>
> "So I say to you: Ask and it will be given to you; seek and you will find; knock and the door will be opened to you. For everyone who asks receives; he who seeks finds; and to him who knocks, the door will be opened.
>
> "Which of you fathers, if your son asks for a fish, will give him a snake instead? Or if he asks for an egg, will give him a scorpion? If you then, though you are evil, know how to give good gifts to your children, how much more will your Father in heaven give the Holy Spirit to those who ask him!" (Luke 11:5-13, emphasis added)

Jesus is inviting us to be bold in our requests! He is inviting us to make BIG requests. He is affirming that when we pray, God hears, and doors open. He is making the point that, just as we would not be stingy with responding to the requests of our own children, He would never be stingy with us, His children.

Here is why I think so many people were profoundly impacted by the story of my illness. We often pray, not believing that God would actually do something BIG, or that we could make truly bold requests. That God can and does the miraculous in our day. But He did, and they saw it, and it changed their understanding of prayer, faith, and God's ability to do BIG things.

Because Mary Ann had heard from God early on that "it will be close, but he will make it," she would not let anyone into my ICU room to pray for me who would not pray for an absolute miracle and total healing. That was a bold move because there was no medical indication that I would pull through.

If Jesus invites bold faith, if He invites BIG requests, we ought to take Him up on His offer. What is it that you need today? Be bold, pray BIG, and wait for a loving Father to answer!

YOUR WILL BE DONE

It can be hard to be bold in our prayer if we are not used to doing this. There is another hard part of prayer: We are to pray boldly and pray BIG, but we are also to pray for God's will to be done (see Matthew 6:10). That is hard, because while God always answers the prayer of faith (see Luke 11:9-10), His perfect answer is not always our perfect answer!

God chose to heal me, twice, in His sovereignty. He does not always do that. That does not mitigate bold and BIG prayer. It requires that we understand that God's perfect will is sometimes unseen by us. Even Jesus, on the eve of His arrest and death, prayed, "'Father, if you are willing, take this cup from me; yet not my will, but yours be done.' An angel from heaven appeared to him and strengthened him. And being in anguish, he prayed more earnestly, and his sweat was like drops of blood falling to the ground" (Luke 22:42-44).

Let that sink in for a long moment.

Jesus was in agony over what was before Him. He pled with His Father to remove the cup of suffering from Him, but even as He prayed boldly and with a BIG request, in the same breath He said, "yet not my will, but yours be done." Did God show up? Yes, an angel from heaven appeared to Him and strengthened Him. Did God remove the path of suffering from Him. No!

A pastor friend of mine was exhilarated when God chose to heal me. He and his congregation had prayed hard, earnestly, boldly, and BIG. He was devastated a few months later when God did *not* heal a young boy in his church who experienced a devastating accident at a youth retreat. This is a man of great faith who has been a model of prayer for me through the years. He was as devastated by God's seeming lack of action as he was thrilled in God's miraculous action in my life.

Reflecting on that event recently he said, "It is amazing how powerful prayer is when we pray in line with God's will." Ultimately, life is not about us but about God. Ultimately, God's eternal purposes are far greater than we can ever comprehend this side of heaven. If Jesus was bound by His Father's will and willing to submit to that will, why would we, His followers and children, be exempt?

Again, we must return to the truth Jesus gave us: "I have told you these things, so that in me you may have peace. In this world you will have trouble. But take heart! I have overcome the world" (John 16:33). We are not exempt from trouble, but we have the promise of God's peace in our situation.

In this regard, one of the most misused verses in Scripture is Romans 8:28. "And we know that in all things God works for the good of those who love him, who have been called according to his purpose." Many assume this means that only good things happen to God's people. Yet just a few verses later Paul asks,

Who shall separate us from the love of Christ? Shall trouble or hardship or persecution or famine or nakedness or danger or sword? As it is written: "For your sake we face death all day long; we are considered as sheep to be slaughtered." No, in all these things we are more than conquerors through him who loved us." (Romans 8:35-37)

Far from denying the reality of bad things, Paul said we should expect them. But know that even in the worst situations, nothing can separate us from God's love. We must understand Romans 8:28 from God's perspective, not ours. This verse is not a promise that life will not come undone. It is a promise that when it does, God has a purpose and a plan that is still good and perfect, and that He can use even our undone*ness* for His greater purposes. God does not remove suffering from our lives, but He *does* redeem that suffering for greater divine purposes.

Bold prayer, prayer that storms the gates of heaven is unapologetic in its requests and BIG in its scope. But it is not bold without praying for God's ultimate will to be done. That is the boldest prayer because that prayer invites God to do what is ultimately best from His perspective, not ours. It is like the prayer of Jesus in the garden—a prayer of deep submission to His perfect will and an invitation for Him to use our lives for His deepest and greatest purposes. That is BOLD prayer. And BOLD faith.

Let me ask you the question that God asks each of us. Are you willing to pray boldly for His will to be done? Do you trust His goodness enough to pray that way? I want to invite you to take that step of ultimate faith and trust right now. Tell Him your need, pray BIG, pray boldly, and boldly invite Him to do His will in your life and situation.

DON'T DO IT ALONE

If I have learned anything through my experiences, it is that we need a "band of brothers and sisters" who will stand with us, pray for us, storm heaven's gates with us, and encourage us. The greatest gift I had on December 4 when I entered United Hospital, and January 4 when I entered Samitivej hospital in Bangkok was a group of faithful prayer partners who took up my cause before the throne of God.

God has given us a wonderful gift in the form of the Internet. Imagine a nonsearchable blog that generated 10,000 unique users over forty-five days. Sites such as CaringBridge make it easy to invite others into your life to intercede on your behalf and to encourage you and your family.

I am sad for those who are so private that they don't invite others in. Not only is it a loss for them, but it is a loss for others who don't have the opportunity to enter into the situation and learn and grow and be changed in the process. People have often thanked us for our transparency over the past several years. They thank us because they can identify with transparency. People cannot identify with facades.

Honesty in our struggles is a gift to others who struggle quietly and wonder if they are alone, different, or somehow have less faith than others. Christ followers are notoriously bad at sharing what is really going on in their lives. If you want transparency go to the local bar, not the local church. That is sad because if anyone should be transparent it is His people, who have nothing to prove and nothing to lose. In fact, the stories of the Old Testament have so much power because they are the real stories of real people: sin, faith, doubt, sorrow, triumph, and the spread of human emotion lived out in real life.

I don't identify with perfect people with perfect lives. First, because they have nothing in common with my life, and second, because I don't believe the perfection is real in their lives either. Mary Ann and I have made the choice to be as authentic and real as we can be about the struggles we have. Of course, we don't reveal everything to everyone, but there are people in our lives who know us intimately. We need others— we know that, and we are not going to live in isolation.

We have two prayer teams: a small, intimate prayer team where we feel free to share information that is not appropriate for a larger audience, that provides prayer and feedback. And a large prayer team where we share most of our lives. I am convinced that I would not even be alive today without those prayer teams! Given the fact that many of the battles we fight in life are spiritual battles, not having a prayer team is going into battle naked, without protection, and deeply vulnerable.

THE STORY BEHIND THE STORY

The Bible tells us about spiritual battles behind the scenes as part of the divine drama being played out between Satan and his forces and the Father and His forces. In the book of Daniel, we find this man of God praying desperately for his people, storming heavens gates with his prayers and petitions.

> In chapter 10, Daniel is praying, fasting, and mourn-ing for the plight of his people who are in captivity—their world had come undone in a very big way. One day he was standing on the banks of the Tigris River (present-day Iraq) in Babylon, and he had a vision of a man "dressed in linen, with a belt of the finest gold around his waist. His body was like chrysolite, his face like lightning, his eyes like flaming torches, his arms and legs like the gleam of burnished bronze, and his voice like the sound of a multitude." (Daniel 10:5-6)

Then this heavenly messenger told Daniel why he had not come sooner:

> Since the first day that you set your mind to gain under-standing and to humble yourself before you God, your words were heard, and I have come in response to them. But the prince of the Persian kingdom resisted me twenty-one days. Then Michael, one of the chief princes, came to help me, because I was detained there with the king of Persia. Now I have come to explain to you what will happen to your people in the future, for the vision concerns a time yet to come. (Daniel 10:12-14)

Even as Daniel had been storming the gates of heaven, God had been at work behind the scenes, but there was a literal struggle between God's emissary and Satan's forces in the unseen world to prevent God's messenger from getting to Daniel. The story behind the story is that there is an unseen world where spiritual forces of good and evil are battling it out, and we are the characters in the drama that they are fighting over: Satan to steal, kill, and destroy, and the Good Shepherd to bring life to the full (see John 10:10).

As Paul reminds us:

> Finally, be strong in the Lord and in his mighty power. Put on the full armor of God so that you can take your stand against the devil's schemes. For our struggle is not against flesh and blood, but against the rulers, against the authorities, against the powers of this dark world and against the spiritual forces of evil in the heavenly realms. (Ephesians 6:10-12)

This is why prayer is so central, so important, and so crucial when life comes undone. We have an adversary who delights in hurting us, sidelining us, taking us out of the game, discouraging us, and destroying us. He is the thief of John 10:10, the one called Satan, who stole the wonderful creation God intended and the fellowship He wanted with us. At the same time, God has heavenly forces at His disposal to help us, encourage us, protect us, and overcome the adversary.

The key to this spiritual battle, this story behind the story, is to understand that life is not random, but we are part of the divine drama of redemption. Therefore, Paul tells us, "Pray in the Spirit on all occasions with all kinds of prayers and requests. With this in mind, be alert [watchful for what Satan is up to] and always keep on praying for all the saints" (Ephesians 6:18).

When I laid in United Hospital battling for my life, the consistent theme of my most intimate prayer partners, who came to St. Paul to pray for me, was that this was not primarily about illness but about a spiritual battle behind the scenes. The only way to fight a spiritual battle is through prayer. Thus the greatest gift we can give one another, as the apostle Paul wrote, is to keep on praying for all of God's people (see Ephesians 6:18).

The evil one thinks he has won when bad things happen to us—when life comes undone. He is counting on the fact that we will respond with bitterness and forsake God—that we will blame God and turn our backs on Him. But every time we respond with faith and trust, he is defeated. Every time we turn toward God in boldness and embrace His will, Satan is proven to be the liar, thief, and fake that he is.

When we, like Job, continue to trust in the face of the destruction of the evil one, he loses face, loses the battle, and God is honored. When we say, like Jesus, "not my will, but yours be done" (Luke 22:42), he is utterly defeated. Every step of faith, every step of trust, every bold prayer is a defeat for Satan and his forces. And God's people all around the world prove that Satan is defeated every day in their faithful walk with God in spite of their circumstances. Each of us is part of that divine drama that will one day defeat Satan and his forces for all eternity.

Understanding the story behind the story—the spiritual realities— changes the equation for our situations. No longer is this just about us. Now it is about our place in a divine drama that will end in the defeat of the evil one and the supremacy of Christ.

The question is whether we will be a part of the triumphal army or cave to the enemy. That is what is at stake when life comes undone and when we face suffering and tough times. Jesus told us that He has overcome the world. I want to join Him in that reality by demonstrating in my life that I am with Him, trust Him, and believe Him. Each time I do that I give the enemy a blow and send him reeling.

One day we will understand how our unique situation fits into the story behind the story, and we will be amazed. And the wonderful thing to know is that Satan has already been defeated—God's D-day was the Cross. But the battle continues until Christ returns and reclaims His creation with His people and creates a new heaven and a new earth. In the meantime, we become the champions of God's power and grace as we trust Him in our own situations.

PRESSING IN

Storming the gates of heaven is sometimes just being quiet and silent and spending time with God. There are times when we need to slow down, decompress, and just be with God. Psalm 46:10 says, "Be still, and know that I am God." Eugene Peterson translates the verse, "Step out of the traffic! Take a long, loving look at me, your High God, above politics, above everything" (MSG).

Here is a counterintuitive principle: When life comes undone it *feels* like we need to work harder, paddle faster, and figure out the solution. But often what is far more important is stripping our lives of distractions and spending time with the only One who can ultimately help us negotiate our personal situation. Often we cannot solve our problems or fix life. But we can rest in the presence of the One who can.

When we take the time to be still and know the Father who loves us with an everlasting love, knows the end from the beginning, knows how He is going to use our situation for His best, and has a plan that we cannot yet comprehend, we start to experience the peace that Jesus talks about in John. In Him we find the quiet, settled confidence that God is in control of all things, that His will is best and that we can rest in our connection to Him.

In my first hospitalization, that is all that Mary Ann and the boys had. As I lay awake in Bangkok, contemplating my odds and dealing with the pain, all I had was time with God. But it was enough!

Life undone is actually an invitation from God to press into Him, the One who cares more about us than anyone else, and the One who wants to give us His peace when nothing about our situation is peaceful. Those who accept the invitation are amazed at how He becomes their peace and gives perspective to their situation. Those who don't accept often end up bitter and alone with a diminished life. In the end, it is not God who moves away, but us.

What does pressing in look like? It means more time with God, spending time in His presence, however you best do that, and more time in His Word. It gives us an eternal and divine perspective on our lives.

It is not complicated, but it takes time and attention. The greatest gift of pain is that it draws us back to the One who is the source of life, the Good Shepherd, who came to give us life and life to the fullest.

BOLD PRAYER

I thank You, Father, that You invite me to pray boldly and with great faith. Because You have invited me, I boldly ask You right now to intervene in the situations I face. I believe You can and will, and I even more boldly pray that You will do so, in Your way, so that Your will is done. Where the evil one is involved behind the scenes, I pray for his defeat. Help me in the midst of my situation to find time to be still and know that You are God, that You are in charge of all things, and that nothing under Your control can ever be out of control. Amen.

QUESTIONS FOR DISCUSSION

Reread Luke 11:5-13. What do we learn about God and prayer in this passage?

How do the twin concepts of praying boldly and praying for God's will to be done come together? Have you ever asked God, as Mary Ann did, "Lord, tell me how to pray in this situation"?

Take another look at Paul's words regarding the "story behind the story" in Ephesians 6:10-12. What can we learn from this about difficulties we sometimes face?

What is your strategy for finding time to just be still before God so that He can minister to your heart and you can be encouraged in His presence?

CHAPTER EIGHT

OFFENSIVE PLAYS
Taking Life Back

Life is lived either on the defensive or the offensive. When life comes undone there is a time when we are living defensively—just hanging on, trying to get our minds around our circumstances, sometimes just trying to survive another hour, or another day. I know; I've been there.

Life undone is deeply disorienting, dislocating our lives and forcing us to deal with our understanding of God. We realize the security we thought we had doesn't exist. It can be deeply exhausting.

But there comes a day when the initial shock has worn off, when survival has turned into coping, and it is time to move from defense to offense. This is not an easy transition. It is far easier to live life defensively. It is sometimes easier to live in our pain than to move beyond our pain. But here is the principle: Christ followers were not meant to live on the defensive, but on the offensive.

Remember what Jesus said in John 10:10: "The thief comes only to steal and kill and destroy; I have come that they may have life, and have it to the full." Choosing to live offensively means deciding that we want the life to the full Jesus offers. Otherwise, we allow the thief to steal that fullness of life and settle for a life diminished, less than it was meant to be.

This was the question faced by Josh and his parents, Jeff and Michelle, after his 2009 skiing accident that left him a paraplegic. The initial weeks after the accident were filled with activity, surgery, dealing with the shock of a life changed forever, a high school graduation, and all the emotions that come with a tsunami change.

As the weeks moved into months, as the shock wore off, as life returned to a semblance of normal, life actually became harder, not easier. The new reality had to be faced on a daily basis. Josh had to learn a new way of living and moving with all the complications of being confined to a wheelchair. Now there was more time to think about losses and uncertainties of the future and why God allowed this to happen.

When the initial shock wears off, what we are left with is fatigue, often depression, anger, sadness, and uncertainty. And we face the question: Will I stay on the defensive, accepting less than can be, or will I go on the offensive and fight for what can be? The journey will be difficult for a while but we can refuse to allow the thief to steal what does not belong to him. Remember, the Good Shepherd came to bring us life and life to the full, regardless of what we have been through.

THE POSTURE OF OUR MIND AND HEART

One of the most significant offensive plays, when life has come undone, is the posture of our mind and heart—what we think about and what our hearts choose to embrace.

Slow down for a moment and consider these words of Paul:

> Rejoice in the Lord always. I will say it again: Rejoice!
> . . . The Lord is near. Do not be anxious about anything,
> but in everything, by prayer and petition, with thanks-
> giving, present your requests to God. And the peace of
> God, which transcends all understanding, will guard
> your hearts and minds in Christ Jesus.
>   Finally, brothers, whatever is true, whatever is noble,
> whatever is right, whatever is pure, whatever is lovely,
> whatever is admirable—if anything is excellent or praise-
> worthy—think about such things. . . . And the God of
> peace will be with you." (Philippians 4:4-9)

Living offensively is not easy. It is easier to live defensively. It is easier to live with our disappointment, anger, depression, and sadness, because that is how we feel when life comes undone. And that is exactly what the thief wants us to do. The choice we make is whether we allow the thief to steal what God intended for us, or whether we push back and say, "NO!" I will not live with a diminished life. I am going to claim what the Good Shepherd wants to give me.

Making that choice starts with what we allow our minds to dwell on. When Paul said, "Rejoice in the Lord always. I will say it again: Rejoice!" he is not giving trite, self-help advice. We have the ONE thing that is most important —no matter what our situation—the personal presence of the living God, with all the blessings He has given us. When I start feeling sorry for myself, all I need to do is to make a mental list of all the blessings I have received from God, and I realize how blessed I really am.

Paul tackles two of the most difficult issues we face when life comes undone: fear and anxiety! These are corrosive to our soul and spirit. The antidote is, "In everything, by prayer and petition, with thanksgiving, present your requests to God" (Philippians 4:6).

Again we are encouraged to storm the gates of heaven with prayer, in a spirit of thanksgiving. The result of an attitude of rejoicing, thanksgiving, and prayer is a radical peace, which Paul acknowledges transcends all human understanding. He says this peace actually guards our hearts and minds. Against what? Against fear and anxiety!

In the last chapter we discussed the importance of pressing into God by taking time to be quiet in His presence. Doing what Paul suggests in this passage requires an intentionality to take time to be with God. That time with Him helps to reorient our minds and hearts away from our fear and anxiety and toward peace and trust. It is a day-to-day challenge, sometimes an hour-to-hour challenge. It is a battle between the thief, who wants us to give in to our situation, and the Good Shepherd, who wants to bring us hope and life in its fullness.

FAITH-FILLED GRIEVING

When life comes undone, there is often grievous loss. That loss needs to be acknowledged and processed, and that takes time—sometimes a long time. The unraveling of my dreams early in my ministry career took a period of ten years to fully heal, so deep were the wounds. We grieve over real losses: physical disabilities, lost dreams, sin that has contributed to our situations either by ourselves or others, and the consequences of living in a fallen world where bad things happen.

In the first year or so after the unraveling, many well-wishing friends gave me advice about "getting back in the saddle" and "letting it go" and "moving on." The truth is they had no idea what I was dealing with inside, the pain I was in, or even the process of healing. When I started medication to deal with depression, some suggested that Christ followers should not be depressed or need medication for depression. In fact, one of the challenges we face when life comes undone is the well-meaning but unhelpful advice of others!

Healthy people grieve losses. They don't gloss them over with spiritual jargon, stuff it deep inside, or put on a façade of joy when the heart is sorrowful. They are honest with themselves, with God, and with others. There are days of gladness and days of sorrow, and the pain of life undone can be triggered in many different ways. Walking by faith when life is hard and hope is scarce is not easy. Like the Lava Lakes trail, it is often hard and steep. The question is not whether we will grieve, but whether we grieve with God, or without God.

Consider this: God shares in our grief. As men and women made in His image, as people who were created for a world without sin and its consequences, He is deeply grieved by what we must walk through. In becoming like us, Jesus has walked in our shoes and understands our pain. Throughout Scripture we encounter the emotions of God—especially His grief over suffering.

Does God experience grief? Think of Jesus weeping at the death of His friend Lazarus, or when He wept in the garden before His arrest. The writer of Hebrews makes this very point:

> During the days of Jesus' life on earth, he offered up
> prayers and petitions with loud cries and tears to the
> one who could save him from death, and he was heard

because of his reverent submission. Although he was a son, he learned obedience from what he suffered. (Hebrews 5:7-8)

God shares your grief. When we grieve, He grieves. When we rejoice, He rejoices. His face is literally turned toward us as His sons and daughters (see Numbers 6:26). We never grieve alone.

I love the Psalms for their honesty of emotions. Psalms 42 and 43 are psalms of deep discouragement. Three times in these psalms we see the refrain:

Why are you downcast, O my soul?
Why so disturbed within me?
Put your hope in God,
for I will yet praise him,
my Savior and my God. (42:5,11; 43:5)

There is loss and grieving, but it is a grieving in faith where the psalmist tells himself in the midst of his grief to put his hope in God. Grief and faith are combined, along with questioning God. Just after these words he questions God,

"I say to God my Rock, 'Why have you forgotten me? Why must I go about mourning, oppressed by the enemy?' My bones suffer mortal agony as my foes taunt me, saying to me all day long, 'Where is your God?'" (Psalm 42:9-10)

Grief, faith, and questioning God: These are all part of processing life that has come undone. The key is that the grief and questions are brought to the feet of Christ "so that we may receive mercy and find grace to help us in our time of need" (Hebrews 4:16). God invites our grief, our tears, our sorrow, and our questions. As we bring our loss and sorrow to Him, He embraces us and brings healing, over time to our wounded souls.

Faith-filled grieving is an offensive move toward healing and reclaiming

our lives. It is grief brought to Christ, where He in turn gives us the mercy and grace we need to reclaim life, one bit at a time. The alternative to faith-filled grieving is grieving without God. When that happens we descend into hopeless grieving rather than hopeful grieving. One leads toward a diminished life, the other toward a hopeful life. One allows the thief to steal our hope, the other puts our hope in the Good Shepherd.

NEVER GIVE UP

Winston Churchill, late in life, was asked to give the commencement address at his former high school where he hadn't made a good impression during his tenure there. He slowly walked to the podium and gave one of the shortest commencement addresses in history. "Never give up! Never, Never, Never, Never, Never."

To give up is to give in to the thief rather than to embrace the plan that the Good Shepherd has for our life (see John 10:10). The thief wants to diminish our lives while the Good Shepherd wants to bring fulfillment to our lives. But we make the choice as to whether we will embrace diminishment, or fulfillment.

A year and a half after my first encounter in the ICU, I am still in physical therapy. It is a hassle, at times painful, and a struggle to get back to the fullest health that I can. I'm not a natural athlete (I hate the gym), so I have to choose to persevere in what I need to do to regain my health.

Regaining our footing after life has come undone is neither easy nor fast. The more it has unraveled, the harder and longer it takes. Whether it is regaining physical or emotional health, doing the work of faith-filled grieving, learning to cope in a wheelchair, raising children alone, living with the loss of a child or spouse—the words of Churchill echo the heart of God, who wants us give us fullness of life, not a diminished life.

A dear friend of mine was just diagnosed with Alzheimer's. His mind is brilliant and his prognosis is scary—especially because he understands the implications. Not for a moment has he thought of giving up. Instead, his letter to me said, "I want to fulfill God's plan for my life in my generation." That is an amazing statement. He is unwilling to settle for anything other than fulfilling God's call on his life, even the uncertain and scary journey of losing his brilliant mind if his condition progresses.

Part of going on the offensive is doing all that we can to press back and regain a sense of wholeness so that we can fulfill God's special plan for our lives. We may have more influence *post* life undone than *pre* undone because of the lessons we have learned, the divine scars we have gained, the ability to empathize with others, and a new perspective on life.

It is exactly for that reason that many who have experienced the dark night of the soul channel their energies into ministries that help others who share their experience. Until that moment when Jesus takes us to heaven, He is not finished with our work on earth. As Paul said, "For we are God's workmanship, created in Christ Jesus to do good works, which God prepared in advance for us to do" (Ephesians 2:10). That was true before our lives came undone, that is true when our lives are undone, and that is true when the pieces come back together. Each of us can learn from my friend, who in the face of his challenge is committed to fulfilling God's plan in our generation!

The apostle Paul had this attitude even after amazing suffering and setbacks in his ministry. He wrote,

> I press on to take hold of that for which Christ Jesus took hold of me. Brothers, I do not consider myself yet to have taken hold of it. But one thing I do: Forgetting what is behind and straining toward what is ahead, I press on toward the goal to win the prize for which God has called me heavenward in Christ Jesus. (Philippians 3:12-14)

I love his words of "straining toward what is ahead" and pressing "on toward the goal." Take a moment right now and reflect on ways that you can press into your situation and cooperate with God in reclaiming your life. If there are things you need to do, I challenge you to press into them with courage and wholehearted energy.

CLEARING THE DECKS

Suffering has a way of focusing the mind. Over the years we accumulate stuff, habits, obligations, and busyness of all kinds. When life comes undone, we rethink what is really important and who is really important—you find out who your real friends are.

We often hear those who have had a close call with death (count me in, twice) talk about how their illness or accident clarified for them what really mattered. They often do some "housecleaning" of life, discarding obligations that were not truly important, refocusing on family and friends, rethinking the use of their time and priorities. As one person said, "Thank you, cancer, for having been in my life." What they were really thankful for was the clarity that the cancer brought to them about what is truly important.

In the wake of my own illnesses, I have intentionally become less busy and more reflective. That has meant a refocusing of what I do and even how I do it. I realize that each day is truly a gift from God and that I am living on borrowed time—I am only here today because of God's miraculous intervention on two desperate occasions. Borrowed time is precious time that I want to use to the greatest advantage both personally and in my work for Christ. As a result, there is a greater richness to life than there was previously, and greater focus for where I expend my time and energy.

Another thing we often accumulate over time is sloppy habits in our relationship with God. Not taking Him seriously, not spending the kind of time with Him that is good for us, and frankly, sinful habits that creep in and seem benign but which rob us of the joy in our relationship with Christ.

Suffering and hardship have a way of reminding us of how central Jesus is to our very existence. It exposes the fault lines of carelessness in our relationship with Him and causes us to rethink habits or practices that keep us from full fellowship with Him. As we noted in chapter two, gifts come in unlikely forms!

If there is ever a time to clear the decks, rethink priorities, refocus our eyes on Christ, and clean house, it is when life has come undone. On the spiritual front, we need Christ desperately—we always did, but our undoneness makes it very clear. On the personal front we have only so much energy, so clearing away accumulated baggage frees us to focus on reclaiming our lives. Given the gift of knowing what is really important, we make an offensive move when we act on that clarity and clear the decks of our lives of all the stuff that is not truly important.

Take a few minutes, perhaps with a pen and note pad and make a list of what is really important to you and what is extra baggage that you could jettison! You will be glad you did.

FORGIVENESS

If life has come undone because of the actions of another, or maybe our own actions, there is nothing more important than forgiving those who have hurt us, and in some cases that means receiving God's forgiveness, and forgiving ourselves.

When Jesus was asked how often we ought to forgive those who have wronged us, His answer was seventy-seven times (see Matthew 18:21-22). In other words, *always* forgive, as many times as needed. Since that is such a hard thing to do, we have to ask ourselves why we would do it—especially to those who have inflicted huge pain in our lives.

We don't do it because they deserve it. They may not deserve it. Ever! But, there are two principles we need to remember, one spiritual and one personal. The spiritual principle is that God chose to forgive us when we did not deserve to be forgiven. We did not deserve His forgiveness, yet He granted it to us fully and completely when we made him the Lord of our lives. Thus Jesus insists that we forgive one another as He forgave us (see Matthew 18:21-35), and do so "from your heart." Jesus actually says that He will not forgive those who refuse to forgive others.

But there is a deeply personal reason to forgive. When we refuse to forgive, we are held hostage by our bitterness until we do. In effect, we are held hostage by the pain inflicted by others and instead of becoming free we become bitter.

I am always reminded of this when family members of homicide victims are interviewed at executions. Sometimes they vow that they will never forgive the one who took the life of their loved one. After the execution they are asked if they feel any better now that justice has been done, and they are just as angry and bitter as before. Not even the death sentence or a life sentence relieves them of their pain and bitterness.

The only way out of the bitterness, the hold that the pain has on our lives, and the anger we feel toward those who hurt us is to choose to forgive them. Not for their sake but for our own sake. I don't pretend it is easy, nor is it quick. But once we have made the decision and practice forgiveness, as the memories come back, the hold of that pain lessens, and we are no longer hostage to those who hurt us.

I shared previously how it took me ten years to completely heal from an early ministry experience where life unraveled. The hardest decision I made in that instance was to forgive those who had hurt us deeply. I had to forgive in my heart many times, but I was not held hostage by bitterness or anger, even though the scars took a long time to heal. Today I am completely free of any residual hurt from what was a desperately painful event. Forgiveness is a journey, but it is a journey of moving toward health and wholeness once again. In those instances where we resist forgiveness, we need to remind ourselves of the proactive forgiveness that God gave to us so that we could know Him.

Sometimes our dark night of the soul is the result of our own sinfulness or foolish actions. The amazing thing about grace is that there is no sin that Christ will not forgive, and there is no situation that Jesus does not want to redeem and use for our growth and His glory.

Only God can take what is bad and redeem it in some way for something good. It has to be deeply frustrating to Satan, as the thief and destroyer, to see God redeem people and situations that he had tried to destroy. As we saw in chapter 4, "Creation Interrupted," Jesus is in the business of redemption, one heart and one situation at a time.

John writes in 1 John 1:9, "If we confess our sins, he is faithful and just and will forgive us our sins and purify us from all unrighteousness." Period! The hard part is often forgiving ourselves! We continue to live with guilt and regret long after God has forgiven us. Although we may have regrets, we need not live with guilt once the Lord of the universe has forgiven us. If He is willing to forgive, we must be willing to forgive ourselves.

There is a phrase I love: "Don't resaw the sawdust." The sawdust is the residual of our sin, now forgiven. Physically you cannot resaw sawdust, but that is what we often try to do time and again by constantly revisiting our sin. We want to learn from our sin, but we cannot wallow in our sin that has been forgiven. The thief, who comes to steal, kill, and destroy, loves it when we try to resaw the sawdust. The Good Shepherd, who comes that we can have life and have it to the fullest, tells us to let it go, for our sin has been covered by His blood spilled on the cross for us! He paid the penalty, and we can move on in forgiveness and grace, learning from our past but pressing into our future.

This offensive move is so important that I encourage you to stop right now for a moment and ask the question: Is there someone I need to forgive for pain inflicted on me? If so, am I willing to take that step? Do I need to ask for God's forgiveness for actions that have helped cause my pain? Or, having done that now or previously, do I need to stop resawing the sawdust and accept the forgiveness and grace that God has already granted me? If your situation requires forgiving others or yourself, there is no real healing until that step has been taken.

THE COURAGE TO CHOOSE WHOLENESS

I have many heroes. They are men, women, young people, and children who have faced life undone but have had the courage to fight back with the conviction that God did not create them for a diminished life but for fullness of life. They have experienced life undone but they did not cave, they pressed into Jesus and into their situation offensively and courageously.

Each time we do that, refusing to let the thief steal what is not his, we claim God's promise of His presence, His power, His peace, and His grace. Over time we gain a perspective that was impossible in the midst of our pain. We emerge changed, people of deeper faith, more focused, and above all, people who have experienced firsthand the grace of God that Mary Ann wrote about in chapter 6. Our immersion in His grace is the greatest game changer of all, and that comes as we press into Him and live on the offensive rather the defensive.

Wherever you are in your process, I encourage you to go on the defensive. Your situation is changed from what it was before life came undone. But God's promise to bring life in fullness is not.

BOLD PRAYER

Father, You are the Good Shepherd, who came so that we can have life and have it to the full. You know the pain I have suffered and the wounds I have received. Now I ask You to heal my life and bring me toward wholeness and healing. Give me the courage to leave behind the wounds of the past and to press into a new future, full of Your grace and presence and power. Amen.

QUESTIONS FOR DISCUSSION

How do you think our attitudes (see Philippians 4:4-9) play into taking our lives back when life comes undone? What strategies have you used to rejoice in the middle of pain?

Life undone brings loss before it brings hope. What can we learn from the example of Christ (see Hebrews 5:7-8) in this process? How did David deal with his losses in Psalm 42?

The apostle Paul experienced a lot of suffering in his ministry. How would you describe his strategy and attitude in Philippians 3:12-14?

This chapter talked about "clearing the decks" of our lives from extraneous stuff so that we can focus on what really matters. Have you experienced this in the midst of suffering? How did "clearing the decks" give you added freedom?

Some deep pain comes from other people—unfairly inflicted on us. What role does forgiveness play in the healing process? Do you have an example of this in your life?

CHAPTER NINE

LIFE REDONE
New Perspectives Forged in Fire

Life is never the same after life undone—but it can be better than it was before. It can be deeper, richer, wiser, more focused, and healthier. Hearts forged by fire are stronger, purer, and deeper!

Three times I have walked through major life undone experiences. What God did in those times was to forge a better me, a me who is more like Jesus, the me He wants me to be. I am still me but a better, gentler, wiser, stronger, godlier, more faithful version of me. In hindsight I would not change those experiences. It was in those hard times that the best of me was forged, purified, and clarified. I like the new me better than the old me. Others do too!

SOUL WORK

Jesus' goal is to take a unique person that He created, with individual gifting and wiring, and through a relationship with Him and the Holy Spirit living within, create a better person—the person that would have been before creation became undone and sin entered the world.

This is the process of stripping our lives of those things that don't reflect the image of God and putting on those things that do.

> You were taught, with regard to your former way of life, to put off your old self, which is being corrupted by its deceitful desires; to be made new in the attitude of your minds; and to put on the new self, created to be like God in true righteousness and holiness. (Ephesians 4:22-24)

The process of putting off those things that are unhealthy and putting on those things that are like Jesus is not an easy process. We see the most progress in this transformation during tough times, when the real us is exposed in all its reality (sometimes ugliness), and we are forced to press into Christ in a deeper, more authentic way because we have nowhere else to turn. That is why we call life undone an unlikely gift.

In the process, God forges the "us" that we were designed and created to be. The person that will have the impact on our world that God wants us to have. The person that is increasingly transformed into the image of Jesus—remember we were originally created in the image of God—so God, through Jesus, is re-creating us in His image. It happens most powerfully in the hard times of life.

My first experience with life undone caused me to enter into a study of God's grace that continues to this day. I moved from being performance oriented in my relationship with God to learning how to live in His gracious grace. That transformation changed my relationship both with God and with others.

I also learned that not all problems are solved this side of eternity. God may choose to not answer my prayers the way I wanted, because He has greater purposes—other ways for me to learn and grow. I learned to trust Him in the face of injustice and pain that I could not solve. This was a painful lesson but one that has given me a deeper perspective on God's purposes in my life.

During my illnesses I learned firsthand that God can do the miraculous, and that I am the recipient of His undeserved grace. That has changed the way I look at every day—as an undeserved gift to be used for Him. I live on borrowed time. In my Thailand experience, staring death in the face, being awake on the ventilator, I learned that I can experience the peace of God and trust Him no matter what the outcome. He was all I had and He was enough.

These are deeply transforming experiences that only come from deep pain and hard times. These transformative experiences are not merely intellectual; they penetrate the deepest part of our lives, which is why they change us. No sermon or book can match the power of transformative experiences forged in pain!

One of the byproducts of deep pain is that it brings to the surface unresolved issues that we have been able to ignore until our pain in another area brings it to the surface. Early in my ministry, after experiencing great pain, I went to see a counselor about issues that had no direction connection to the situation I faced, but the pain brought them to the surface. It is always a blessing when unresolved areas of life come to our attention because dealing with them helps us become the person God wants us to be. Never ignore what pain reveals.

As I look back on times when life has come undone, times that were excruciatingly hard and painful in the process, I realize that all the major growth and transformative experiences of my life came in those times and their aftermath. Painful as they were, how can I be anything but grateful to God for the opportunity to experience transformation that never would have happened without them? And in the process I have participated in the "fellowship of sharing in his sufferings, becoming like him in his death, and so, somehow, to attain to the resurrection from the dead" (Philippians 3:10-11).

As life is redone, as it comes back together for you, pay close attention to the transformation that has taken place in your life. Places where God has made Himself better known to you, lessons you have learned. Pay attention and think about them because these are precisely the transformative experiences He wants for *you,* so that *you* become a better *you,* as God's character and purposes become a greater part of your life.

Whether or not you journal, I would encourage you to put down on paper the lessons you have learned and the transformation you have experienced. Remember, these are the most significant opportunities for you to experience the spiritual transformation God wants for each of us. The more you pay attention to what God is doing in your heart, and cooperate with that work He is doing, the more you gain from having been in the heat of His forge.

I have in my home study a two-thousand-year-old beautiful piece of pottery, a bowl from an ancient grave in central China. It looks pristine, with a grey patina. It is the kind of piece that one might see in a museum. Except, undetectable to the eye, this wonderful bowl is actually broken, and if you gently dismantle it, it exists in five pieces. It looks perfect, but it has been cracked and damaged.

I love those cracks because it reminds me of my life. People may look at me and think, he has it all together, but my life has cracks, divine scars that have made me who I am. So does yours. Those cracks and scars revealed areas where transformation needed to take place and where you experienced God's work, so wear those scars and cracks with pride. God used them and redeemed them for His purposes in our lives.

A friend of mine, who has walked through several periods of serious illness, made an interesting observation about scars. She said sometimes we think they are scars but in reality they are scabs that have not completely healed. The scab comes off at an unexpected time, and we need to again address that wound, again opened. How true. Deep pain does not just go away. When it returns, we again turn to Christ and allow Him to work in our hearts. It is often like that with forgiveness, traumatic injuries we have received, the loss of a loved one, or a great injustice we have suffered. Each time the scab comes off we again have the opportunity to relearn and practice a transforming lesson.

It is a great gift for those who have experienced life undone to be transparent with others about their experiences. Many around us are struggling with private pain, but don't know who to talk to, or are afraid to be transparent. Our willingness to be real about the situations we have faced or are facing is an encouragement to those who are struggling silently. It opens a conversation and brings the ability to minister to others who are hurting. Our transparency and honesty encourages the same from others.

DEPTH

Much of life is lived on the surface, superficially, accidentally, and without deep thought. People are often busy, distracted, and unfocused. Those who have suffered deeply, whose lives have been transformed in the process, display a depth of life and thinking that is radically different from the norm. If you are one of those, you have been given a great gift and God wants to use that gift to influence others.

There is nothing like faith, forged in suffering. Each of the faith heroes of Hebrews 11 had a suffering-forged faith that gave them an unshakable trust and confidence in the living God, and they were therefore willing to suffer and even die for Him. They displayed a perseverance and resolve that was unusual. Speaking of Moses it says, "He persevered because he saw him who is invisible" (Hebrews 11:27). If God has met you in your pain, you, too, have seen Him who is invisible; you have felt His presence and experienced His love and grace.

That depth should have a direct impact on our jettisoning the sin that we have allowed to linger in the shadows of our lives. We exchange that sin for a wholehearted, nonnegotiated followership of Jesus. Why continue to live with the junk when we have experienced the fellowship of Jesus in a new way and been recipients of His generous grace? To do so is to negate the very lessons that God made possible for us to learn through our pain.

Depth is the opposite of superficial. Most lives are lived superficially due to a lack of deep thinking about what is truly important: how to orient our lives around that which is eternally significant. What became starkly evident to me in those times of life undone is how much of life is superficial and how little I cared about the superficial when in pain. Why? Because ultimately the superficial things were not important to my life, but it took the pain to differentiate between what was really important and what was not.

One of the takeaways from life undone is that we no longer need to live with the superficial but can focus our lives around what is truly important. That is a gift, and it leads to a deeper and more productive, significant life if we carry those lessons over into our redone lives. Suffering draws us away from superficiality and into depth, away from the trivial to the important. Life undone is a time of separating the unimportant from the important and the significant from those things that are really insignificant.

The writer to the Hebrews put it well:

Therefore, since we are surrounded by such a great cloud of witnesses, let us throw off everything that hinders and the sin that so easily entangles, and let us run with perseverance the race marked out for us. Let us fix our eyes on Jesus, the author and perfecter of our faith, who for the joy set before him endured the cross, scorning its shame, and sat down at the right hand of the throne of God. Consider him who endured such opposition from sinful men, so that you will not grow weary and lose heart." (Hebrews 12:1-3)

Our pain reveals what is truly important. It reveals parts of our character that need transformation. It reveals sin that we have allowed to linger. Pain is the great revealer of sin, character, and dysfunction. Therefore it is an opportunity to deal with those areas God wants us to deal with. Not to do so is to lose a great opportunity to "throw off everything that hinders and the sin that so easily entangles" so that we can "run with perseverance the race marked out for us."

Peter writes about the connection between suffering and sin: "Therefore, since Christ suffered in his body, arm yourselves also with the same attitude, because he who has suffered in his body is done with sin. As a result, he does not live the rest of his earthly life for evil human desires, but rather for the will of God" (1 Peter 4:1-2). This is one of those unexpected gifts that suffering brings to our lives.

Don't short-circuit the opportunity to grow through authentic attention to the sin that your pain reveals. This is a part of God's work, and it is required for those who desire to go deep with Him.

The spiritual depth and the faith lessons you have gained through pain are a gift to be used in ministry to others. Faith and following Jesus are often shallow and superficial in the church today. Those whose faith has been forged in fire and pain experience the presence of God with a depth that others need to know about. If you are transparent, others will gravitate to you when they face trouble because they know you have been there, that you understand, that you have a depth of understanding that they need.

To put it another way, those who have suffered much have much more ministry capital to share with others. Don't neglect your capital. It is one of our obligations as life becomes redone. We have a gift that God desires us to give away.

With depth of faith comes depth of compassion. Compassion and empathy were not part of my original wiring. They are today! The pain I have experienced, emotionally, spiritually, relationally, and physically, over the years has softened my heart and given me a great compassion for others who are hurting. Again, it's a part of the spiritual transformation in my life forged through pain. One cannot suffer without becoming more sensitive to the suffering of others.

That is why Paul said that as we suffer, the comfort of Jesus overflows into our lives so that it can in turn overflow into the lives of others. We cannot give away what we have not experienced (see 2 Corinthians 1:3-7). But what we have experienced we can share with a tenderness and authenticity and compassion that is borne out of God's grace in our own lives.

One of my own convictions coming out of times of pain is that I have an obligation to look for and come alongside other hurting people. Not everyone can do that well. Those who have suffered can! That applies to hurting people in the church and hurting people who don't yet know Jesus. We become the heart of Jesus when we encourage and minister to others who are walking through pain.

REFOCUSED LIVES

Suffering clarifies what is important in life—what really matters. Who really matters! Clearly, Jesus is the primary focus of our lives, and if we needed Him in the painful times, we also know that we need Him when the pain dissipates. Once we have tasted His presence in a new way, why would we want to leave that gift behind? Life undone has given us a gift of a deeper relationship with Christ. When life starts to be redone, it is time to build on that intimacy and fellowship and not allow it to dissipate. This means spending more time with God, in whatever way you best connect with Him, in prayer, in reading His Word, in continuing the transformation process that your painful event initiated. There is no more important focus of our lives than becoming close to Christ, but it sometimes takes a crisis to realize that truth.

Life undone also develops a new, deeper dependence on God. After all we have seen Him work faithfully in our pain, why settle any longer for a mere superficial dependence on Him? Why not press into Him in a new way on a daily basis for all of our needs, for His direction, and for His personal presence in our day? When I said that life redone can be better than it was before life undone: deeper, richer, wiser, more focused, and healthier, much of that richness comes from a new focus on those things that are important and a deeper relationship with the Father.

Life undone also affects our relationships with one another. Pain and suffering have a tendency to reveal who our real friends are. Superficial friendships are common both in and outside the church. When I went into the hospital on December 4, 2007, for forty-two days, our family discovered a lot about the depth of friendships we had, and those friendships sustained our family in an amazing way. All too often, we find, however, that those who called themselves friends are nowhere to be found when suffering hits. Or they are moralistic friends like those that Job had giving him unhelpful, discouraging, and unbiblical advice.

As a result of our own pain, we have intentionally developed a set of friends we call "Friends for Life." They are the kinds of friends who give depth to our lives, whose own lives are such that they challenge us to grow, people who encourage and love unconditionally. We place great emphasis in our schedules to spend time with these true friends. We want to do life with them; we want to be there for them. We cultivate these friendships as one of our most precious gifts.

Life undone demonstrates the need for faithful, godly, intimate friendships because when life is hard and hope is scarce, they are the loving touch of Christ to us and us to them. Superficial friendships cannot provide that kind of support. Friends for life can!

Pain also causes us to look more closely at our own personal priorities and how we spend our time and energy. Time is the one commodity that we can never get back. When life is stripped bare by pain, we become aware that there are many extraneous activities and obligations that have little relevance to our lives. Life redone is a time to evaluate what we put back into our lives, what is really important, what will leave a lasting legacy.

This was especially poignant for me coming out of two near-death experiences, reminding me daily that I live on borrowed time. It has led me to think more critically about how I invest that time with family, friends, work, and ministry. I care more deeply today about how I can influence others for Jesus and help them become all that they can be.

After life redone, in small and large ways our hearts, perspectives, and situations have changed. We pray differently, relate to God more intimately, prioritize in new ways, care more deeply about some things and less deeply about others. God has taken us through a priceless process of refocusing our lives around those things that are most important, and revealing the superficial for what it is. Our hearts have been reforged through fire. In pain, we have been reshaped into a more authentic version of the person God created. That is a gift.

LIVING IN HOPE RATHER THAN REGRET

There are losses and gains in life. Sometimes gains come out of losses as God redeems the loss in ways that we could not expect. The question is whether we will focus on the loss and live in regret, or embrace the gains and live in hope. The choice we make defines our future and determines our attitude.

I remember talking to Mary Ann after my forty-two-day life-and-death struggle in United Hospital. I asked her, "Do you regret what happened?" She was quiet a long moment and then said, "No, but I never want it to happen again." We could not anticipate then that it would and this time in another country. But her answer was instructive. We learned so much about God, prayer, His power, and His presence during that long ordeal that we would not trade the experience for anything. God did something life changing in us through our pain. Our hearts were reforged and it was a gift to us.

I do not want to assume that your answer would be the same. Many suffer because of the evil of others, such as sexual abuse, and would never give the answer Mary Ann did in our case. But, no matter how bad the wound, part of how God redeems our pain is in what we learn about Him in the process. Only God can take what is horrendous and redeem it in ways that are so improbable. He is not the author of our pain, but He can and does redeem our pain.

Yes, there have been losses. I struggle with energy and fatigue. My travel has been severely curtailed. My work days are shorter. I am still in physical therapy for soft tissue in my legs and feet that hardened in the ICU. As a friend of mine says, "I *have* been compromised." While I am fighting back to regain full health, there may be a new normal that I have to live with.

But when I consider the gains of a reforged heart, of the soul work God did in the process of the past two years, those gains so far outweigh the loss. The gains are painful gifts with divine scars that have reshaped us. But the gains have eternal value while the losses have temporary value.

As you think about your life redone, whatever the life undone situation you have faced, I would urge you to consider the gains that have come in the midst of your pain. Each gain, each reshaping of your heart and soul, each reprioritizing of your life is a gift to a more authentic you. God took what was painful and redeemed it for something precious and eternal in your life.

If you are still in the process of grieving your loss, I understand. Healing takes time, sometimes a lot of time. But, in the process, be sensitive to gains that God reveals to you in your loss, ways your heart and life or your relationship with Him are being reshaped. If you are watching, you will start to see gains and not just loss.

The largest gain for any of us is a new understanding of the love, mercy, grace, and presence of God. At the end of the day, He is what we need no matter what our situation. Unlike the thief who comes to steal, kill, and destroy, He came that we might have life, and life to the fullest.

Life to the fullest is not about perfect health, plenty of money, or a life without pain. It is all about experiencing the peace, joy, and purpose that comes from a life full of God. A life full of God is available to everyone—no matter what our life situation. If through loss we find a life full of God, that is the greatest gift we could ever receive. And a life full of God is a life of hope rather than regret. Which life are you living?

BOLD PRAYER

I thank You, Lord, for taking me through times of suffering because as I look back, You have reshaped my heart, life, and priorities through them. And, I know in a new way how faithful You are and how deeply You love and how generous Your grace. Thank You for using pain in my life to mold my heart after Yours and to deepen my relationship with You. You loved me enough to allow me to suffer, and through that pain You reshaped my soul. Amen.

QUESTIONS FOR DISCUSSION

How have pain and suffering reshaped your perspective on life, priorities, and relationships?

Personal and spiritual depth is shaped in the fire of life. What are the markers of those who have been deeply shaped by God in Hebrews 12:1-3? How have these markers been evident in your life?

How does pain or suffering actually contribute to a life of fullness and joy? What lessons have you learned in life that could not have been learned apart from the challenges you encountered?

CHAPTER TEN

FREEDOM
Reshaped Hearts

Life lived with God is a journey to freedom. It is a journey from selfishness to selflessness, from sin to righteousness, from facades to authenticity, from living by the expectations of others to that of pleasing an audience of One, from our sinful nature to a life in the Spirit. Every step toward freedom is a step in the right direction. Jesus said, "So if the Son sets you free, you will be free indeed" (John 8:36). Freedom in Christ is a wonderful place to live.

As citizens of a world that has been interrupted by Satan, we are held captive by many things: pride, independence, materialism, success, self-sufficiency, the expectations of others, sinful habits, distractions from those things that are most important, and selfish hearts.

Every time one of these *captive makers* is stripped from our lives we become more free, more like the person God created us to be, and our hearts more like His. In a divine reversal, what we consider to be the ultimate disaster can, in fact, be a *freedom maker*.

Once I have experienced a great failure, I no longer need to worry about failing. Once I have lost my self-sufficiency, I no longer need to try to be self-sufficient and am free to rely on God. Being stripped of our pride gives us the freedom to receive from others when we need it. No longer do we have the need to be self-sufficient in all things.

After experiencing life undone in its many versions, I can let go of my pride—I am forced to, and it is freeing. Now I can just be me! No longer do I need to pretend I am something I am not. I am free to live with authenticity.

When I have not lived up to the expectations of others, I realize that not only can I not pull that off but I don't need to. Another step toward freedom! The pain of suffering clarifies those things that are not really important in my life that I can release without guilt, and I am free to focus on what is truly important.

In thousands of ways, large and small, life undone points us toward Christ, faith, trust, humility, and a freedom. Ironically, life undone contributes to a life of freedom.

That is where we want to end our journey both in this book and in our personal lives. In freedom!

THE GIFT OF HUMILITY

Suffering helps to free us from the pride that enslaves us and in turn grows humility like nothing else can. Pride is both a mask of pretense and a spirit of the heart. As a mask, it is pretending that we are something we are not, know more than we do, are more competent than we are. As a spirit of the heart, it is believing that we are self-sufficient and are better than we are. Both the mask and the heart posture are sinful. They hold us hostage as we struggle to keep up the pretense.

Suffering has a wonderful way of stripping away pride. When life comes undone we can't pretend we are sufficient anymore. We are forced to acknowledge our need for God and for others. Our weakness becomes our strength.

The apostle Paul, that great giant of the faith, also had to learn humility the hard way. Listen to his story:

> To keep me from becoming conceited because of these surpassing great revelations, there was given me a thorn in my flesh, a messenger of Satan, to torment me. Three times I pleaded with the Lord to take it away from me. But he said to me, *"My grace is sufficient for you, for my power is made perfect in weakness."* Therefore I will boast all the more gladly about my weaknesses, so that Christ's

power may rest on me. That is why, for Christ's sake, I delight in weaknesses, in insults, in hardships, in persecutions, in difficulties. *For when I am weak, then I am strong.* (2 Corinthians 12:7-10, emphasis added)

The words of Jesus to Paul are amazing and compelling for anyone who has walked the path of pain. "My grace is sufficient for you, for my power is made perfect in weakness." Ironically, the path to power is found in weakness. We are truly strong when we are forced to rely on God for His grace and power. This gives new meaning to wearing our divine scars with pride. It is why Paul says, "For when I am weak, then I am strong."

We are strong when we humbly rely on God for His grace and power. We are weak when we rely on ourselves. Suffering frees us from self-reliance and makes us strong through Christ. No longer do we need to pretend we are sufficient. No longer do we have to pretend we are something we are not. We can just be who we are in our strengths and weaknesses, humbly relying on God.

Suffering creates humility because we have come to the end of ourselves and are forced to give up our illusions of control. Life undone is life out of control for us. But that is when we learn that God is in control and nothing under God's control can ever be out of control!

Ironically, one of the most freeing moments of my life was the day I packed up my moving van, after what I considered, at the time, a failed pastorate. I had never experienced failure; I had never had life come undone before. Everything I had tried I had succeeded at. This time it did not go as planned. Now, with what I considered a failure I no longer had to prove I couldn't fail. I already had. The train had come off the rails. Never again did I need to worry about failing!

Having had two long bouts in the ICU, I can say with candor that if you were not humble on the way in, you certainly are on the way out! There is no dignity in being sick, in having tubes sticking into your body, no control over bodily functions, wearing the dubious gown, and being totally at the mercy of others. Illness reveals the fragility of our bodies—as does old age, when our bodies slowly betray us, and the "clay pots" the apostle Paul calls our earthly bodies crack and crumble.

It was humbling to go to physical therapy after my first long hospital stay and learn how to walk and balance again after thirty-six days in bed. Or occupational therapy, where they wanted me to count money and take timed tests of motor function, which I failed miserably. Or speech therapy, where they tested my cognitive skills and memory (flunked there as well). I still have days of brain fog, where the neurons don't seem to connect very well.

I have a saying that sums up some of my feelings: Nothing to prove, nothing to lose. That is how I want to live life. God made me who I am, He wired me the way He did, He has given me a special work to do for Him. I don't have to prove that I am anything other than who He made me to be, and if I have nothing to prove, I have nothing to lose when I fail or don't live up to someone's expectations. That is freedom!

Ironically, when I started to wake up from my coma at United Hospital, I kept saying "Nothing to prove, nothing to lose." I knew that if there was ever a time to practice that mantra, it was then, when I was at my weakest.

Being stripped of our pride frees us to accept the help and love of others, something that many of us find hard to do. In the aftermath of my illness, we have been the recipients of a great deal of love and help. For me, as with most, it is easier to give than to receive, but the grace and humility to receive is a gift that all of us need.

This is the route to personal authenticity—a commodity in short supply in today's world. Pretense is a lie. It is also hard to keep up. Authenticity is honesty about who we are and what we struggle with and the challenges we face. Others are drawn to authenticity because it is real, and not many people are real. Authenticity also leads to a new way of thinking about who we need to please.

AN AUDIENCE OF ONE

Have you ever thought about how much time and energy we expend in trying to live up to the expectations of others? Authenticity means that we no longer need to work to prove something, but we can simply be who God made us to be. Our highest goal is not to please people but to please an audience of One—our Father. Again, that is freedom!

With humility comes a "nothing to prove, nothing to lose" view of life, which leads to authentic living. Authentic living is about being who God created us to be and not someone else's version for us, whether they be our parents, our in-laws, or others. The question is no longer, what I have to do to please other people, but what I need to do to please God.

I remember the pressure I felt as a young pastor to be whatever a pastor is supposed to be. I put expectations on myself, and others put expectations on me, and pretty soon it was hard to be me. I worried too much about what people would think about me. I took criticism too deeply. I felt like a failure too often. I had something to prove and a lot to lose, which is not a fun way to live life. Life undone has stripped much of that out today, which is wonderful and freeing.

My main question today is, What do I need to do to please the Father? Not only will I never please everyone else, but that is not the call on my life—or yours. Pleasing the Father is my calling. His priorities for my life, time, energies, and heart are what count. He is the One we will give account to one day. No one else's opinions will matter on that day.

Life undone has a way of clarifying what is really important. It causes us to ask the ultimate questions and resolve life issues. God and His plan for our lives are the really important issues. Living at the intersection of God's call for our lives, and our embracing that call, is crucial. We now have the freedom to live the life He has for us, not follow the opinions of others.

COURAGEOUS RESOLVE

Suffering develops courage, and courage gives us the freedom to live out God's call for us. There is a flint-like quality to those who have walked through life-undone experiences, because they have endured hardship and experienced suffering. Frequently, when I go in for a medical test, the personnel will apologize for either the indignity or the discomfort. My response is that they cannot do anything worse to me than has already been done (not completely true but close enough).

I think of my friends who endured through long cancer treatments. Their courage is amazing and their faith is strong. It has been forged in fatigue, discomfort, uncertainty, and just trying to gather the strength to make it through another day.

I think of those who have had to deal with the trauma of sexual abuse as youngsters, and the courage it takes to confront such evil, and believe that God is still good. I think of friends whose lives have been maligned by untrue words and gossip and who have had to leave their reputations in the hands of God—and trust Him for vindication.

The most courageous people I know are people who have walked through deep suffering of one kind or another. Their faith, perseverance, and courage were forged in those dark times.

But the courage that was forged brings freedom. No longer do we need to live cautiously. No longer do we need to live in fear. The worst, from our perspective, has already happened. We now know what is really important. We are living to please the audience of One.

For those who have dealt with serious illness, there is also the new realization that life is short and precious, and that we live on borrowed time. I certainly do! I take seriously Moses' prayer to "Teach us to number our days aright, that we may gain a heart of wisdom" (Psalm 90:12). Every day to me is precious, and I want to use each day in a way that contributes to God's purpose for me on this earth.

This ought to lead us to live with a kind of reckless abandon for the cause of Christ. Freed of our need to impress, free of our facades, free of our pride, free of the need to live up to others expectations—we are free to follow God more closely, depend on Him more deeply, and live with reckless abandon. We have nothing to lose and everything to gain!

If He has given us dreams, we are free to pursue them knowing that there is nothing better than being in the center of His will. If He has been calling us out of our comfort zone in some area, we are free to get out of our boat, like Peter, and follow!

In many instances God uses our suffering to minister to others who have suffered in similar ways. We are free to use the overflow of His comfort to comfort those who are floundering with life undone. If God gives you the burden to help others who hurt, you become an agent of hope and healing. There is nothing more gratifying than to channel our hard-earned lessons into the grace others need to negotiate their pain.

One might think that those who have had life come undone are pessimistic and discouraged people. There are certainly times in the process where that is the case. But many of the most optimistic people I know have suffered the most deeply. They have learned that God can be trusted, that God is a good and gracious friend, and that there is always hope. In retrospect we also know that the lessons we learned and the reforming of our hearts would not have happened any other way. Often, in the light of time we can see that the gains can outweigh the losses.

Divine scars deepen faith, create courage, and forge an optimism that God is at work, is still in control, and is redeeming a broken world, and we have the proof because He has done it for us! No one who has been touched by God's grace and presence can be honestly pessimistic. If God is at work, bringing redemption to His interrupted creation through His work in individual lives, how can we not be encouraged? Sure there is a lot of bad news, but God is good news and He trumps the bad news because He has overcome the world, and we can have peace even though we face trouble.

As I travel the world and meet Christians who are persecuted, harassed, have had their homes and churches burned, have been beaten and thrown in jail, I am always amazed at their smiling faces and optimistic spirits. They have no doubt that God is greater than the adversary, that He is all powerful, that they can trust Him and their love for Him, and His cause is amazing given what they have faced. We in the West have little conception of what many Christ followers face every day of their lives.

Their joy and peace in the face of poverty, persecution, and all the challenges of life is proof of what Christ told His disciples, "I have told you these things, so that in me you may have peace. In this world you will have trouble. But take heart! I have overcome the world" (John 16:33).

They have been recipients of the unlikely gift and know that it is a wonderful thing to come to the place where they have nowhere else to turn but God. Because in those times He has proven Himself to be everything they need. They have been touched by His divine touch, they have experienced the overflow of His comfort, and His peace is evident in their lives.

Had I not become sick, I would never have experienced His touch as I did. Had I not walked through deep pain early in my career, I would not have experienced the amazing grace of God in my life, which has shaped my life since then. I have been the recipient of mercy, grace, God's touch, and deep spiritual insights through my life-undone experiences. I would not trade the pain for His touch, which has changed my life and brought me closer to Him. His touch changes our hearts and gives us great courage.

Courage is all about the willingness to live out God's call on our lives with resolve and without reserve. It is an all-in attitude and it is forged in the furnace of trial. Take a moment and consider the ways that you have become a free person through your life-undone experience. How has God reshaped your heart? How are you different? How has it changed your outlook on life? Life undone is deeply painful, but the freedom it can bring is a wonderful gift.

That freedom comes directly out of a relationship with God and His work in our hearts. If you have read this book but do not have a personal relationship with the One who created you in His image, who loves you with an amazing and everlasting love, and who wants to give you His peace—now, and for eternity, I invite you to stop right now and ask Him to come into your life. It is the most important invitation you will ever respond to. He is the answer to life undone and He wants you to be a part of His family. He is waiting for you.

CLAIMING OUR LEGACY

What is the real legacy of life-undone experiences? As we respond in faith and trust, the legacy is a *reshaped heart* that looks more like God's heart than it did before. Think about that: Through our painful experiences, our hearts have been reshaped to be more like God's heart!

The very goal of our lives as Christ followers is to become like Christ. And in the most painful experiences we could encounter, He redeems our pain by reshaping our hearts so that they look more like His. Through our brokenness we learn to walk by faith and rely on Him for what we need moment by moment. In our pain we are stripped of our pride and learn humility. In suffering we learn to be compassionate toward others who suffer and the overflow of God's comfort to us overflows from us to them.

Life undone clarifies what is truly important and calls us away from the superficial. It creates in us a more authentic life that plays to the audience of One. It strips us of distractions and sinful habits. In all of these ways, and in many individual ways, it reshapes our hearts in ways that are consistent with His heart. And in the process we become more like the person that He created us to be.

Is that a gift? I believe it is one of the greatest gifts we could ever receive. Not the pain of life undone but the heart that God creates in us through the process of dealing with our pain. Can you thank God today for the legacy of a reshaped heart formed in the forge of your pain? Wear your divine scars with pride. They represent new character, reshaped hearts, and courage that cannot be forged except through fire. We discover the grace and strength of God in our need and our weakness.

BOLD PRAYER

Father, I thank You today for all the ways You have been faithful to me through my pain. I claim my legacy of a reshaped heart and pray that it will continue to become more like Your heart. I thank You for character, courage, and greater life clarity that have come through fire. Give me what I need today. Amen.

QUESTIONS FOR DISCUSSION

Why did God not heal Paul's infirmity and how did that "unlikely gift" mold Paul's character and faith (see 2 Corinthians 12:7-10)? How have your "unlikely gifts" molded your character, humility, and faith?

How have your "life undone" experiences actually brought greater freedom to your life?

All of us are shaped by our story and biography, and God uses the events of our lives, good and bad, to shape us. As you look back over your life, how have the difficult times shaped you into who you are today? What would be different in your life if you had not walked through these times?

We wrote about "claiming our legacy" as God's children. In what ways has your perspective on suffering changed through reading this book?

AFTERWORD

We are all on a personal journey toward wholeness in Jesus. If this book has been helpful to you, or you have insights you would like to share, we would love to hear from you. You can reach us at tjaddington@gmail. com.

ABOUT THE AUTHORS

T.J. Addington is the international ministry leader of the EFCA, organizational consultant, speaker, and author. He resides in Minnesota with his wife of thirty-five years, Mary Ann. They are the parents of two children, Jon and Steven (Chip). In their spare time they enjoy reading, traveling, writing, and fly-fishing. T.J. is the author of three previous books, *High-Impact Church Boards; Leading from the Sandbox: Develop, Empower, and Release High-Impact Ministry Teams;* and *Live Like You Mean It.* T.J.'s passion is to see God's people be all that they can be.

Mary Ann is a mom and nurse, who loves to minister to hurting people.

NOTES

INCLUDES QUESTIONS FOR BOARD DISCUSSION

T. J. ADDINGTON

HIGH IMPACT CHURCH BOARDS

How to Develop
Healthy, Intentional, and Empowered
Church Leaders

ALSO BY T.J. ADDINGTON

T. J. ADDINGTON

LEADING
from the
SANDBOX

How to Develop, Empower, and Release
High-Impact Ministry Teams

Foreword by John Ortberg

T. J. ADDINGTON

LIVE
LIKE YOU
MEAN IT

The 10 Crucial Questions That Will Help You

- Clarify Your Purpose

- Live Intentionally

- Make the Most of the Rest of Your Life

BY GORDON ADDINGTON

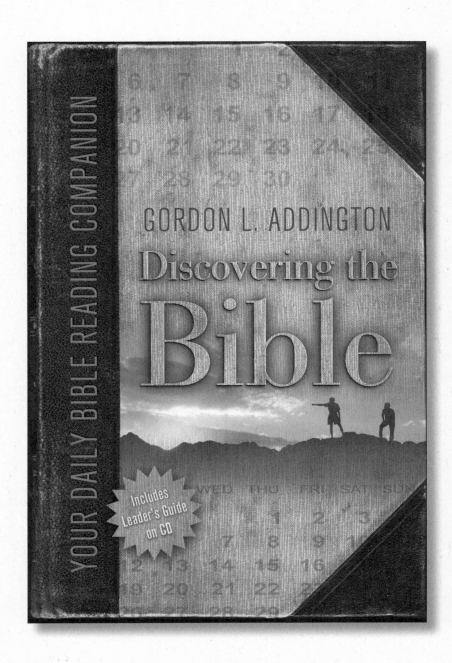